I AM COMING SOON

THE WORDS OF JESUS

MELODY FORREST
FOREWORD BY DR. E. MARSHALL BLALOCK

Copyright © 2020 Melody Forrest.

All rights reserved. No part of this book may be used or reproduced by any means, graphic, electronic, or mechanical, including photocopying, recording, taping or by any information storage retrieval system without the written permission of the author except in the case of brief quotations embodied in critical articles and reviews.

Photo by Dr. R. Marshall Blalock "Fishing Boat on the Sea of Galilee"
Edited by Marcia Cornell

Scripture quotations taken from The Holy Bible, New International Version® NIV® Copyright © 1973 1978 1984 2011 by Biblica, Inc. TM. Used by permission. All rights reserved worldwide.

Bible Reading Plans and Journal of Jesus's Words

Two plans:
One Strictly New Testament,
One with Old Testament References

"Now the Bereans were of more noble character
than the Thessalonians,
for they received the message with great eagerness and
examined the Scripture every day to see if what Paul said was true."

Acts 17:11 NIV

Foreword

People long for truth, but finding it seems elusive in the post-modern world. This journal is unique, because the reader is invited to discover truth in the words of Jesus Christ. He said it himself (John 18:37), "The reason I was born and came into the world is to testify to the truth." This is not any book, not just any journal. This is a step into the truth of Jesus in his own words. Let them sink in, let his word inspire and convict you. Let the parables come to life as you read them. If you want to know the truth, and especially if you want to follow Jesus, the first step is to listen to his voice. You won't regret even one minute of the time you spend here...so take your time.

Once you go through the words of Jesus, you will be asked to take a second look, this time through the lens of the Hebrew scriptures. In studying the Bible, the most important interpretive tool is context, and the original hearers all knew the Old Testament well. These passages provided the context for so much of what Jesus taught his disciples. The author of this journal is asking you to consider the words of Jesus in the context of the Old Testament, the written word of the day. You may find other passages to provide this context, but for the sake of this journal, the author has chosen some to get you started. Of course we have the epistles and so much more to teach us, but Melody Templeton reminds us wisely, the place to begin is with the words of our Savior.

As a pastor, there is one goal that is always in front of me: Point people to Jesus. I am grateful for Melody Templeton putting this journal in place, because it points the reader squarely to Jesus. She writes not from an Ivory Tower, but from a heart longing to love and follow Jesus. Reading through the words of Jesus is not always easy, but it is always good. I invite you to the journey of a lifetime, to meet Jesus.

--

Dr. R. Marshall Blalock, Pastor
First Baptist Church
48 Meeting Street | Charleston SC 29401

Why Jesus's Words?

One day I was asked, "If you could time travel, where would you go?" I quickly answered, "Sermon on the mount to hear Jesus live." I would love to experience His Words. But then I realized, I had the transcription.

I decided to read through the red letters of the New Testament. I thought it would be fun and easy. Boy, was I wrong. I stopped reading midway through Mark. Concentrating on Jesus's words without the commentary was difficult. He is demanding and precise. He is loving beyond all measure and He expects us to act like him. I had to change my view of The Christ and look deeper into who I was as one of His followers.

Please do not enter into this reading lightly. Spend time in prayer, petitioning the Holy Spirit for wisdom before each read. You will have to re-read many passages and you may still not understand the meaning. Journal and pray on those confusing passages and ask for insight, but keep reading.

Do not skip to the plan with the Old Testament references. It is important that **you read Jesus's Words alone first**. You must let Jesus talk directly to you before you study the prophesies and Jewish mindset of His time.

You may find, like myself, you need to stop. Give it time and wait for the Holy Spirit to nudge you to return. It took my third try to get through them. Be patient with yourself and allow the words to change you. This is not an academic journey, but a spiritual one. These words will and should change you. Be open to that change and greater understanding of God's purpose of sending Jesus to us. Only God knows where you are in your journey. Let Jesus's words guide you to the destination God has planned for you.

> "When your words came, I ate them; they were my joy and my heart's delight,
> for I bear your name, O Lord God Almighty." Jeremiah 15:16

Don't just read Jesus' Words, eat them! They will nourish your soul.

- Melody

The Gospels

Matthew

The Gospel of Matthew was written by the Jewish tax collector Matthew (called Levi prior to his calling). Tax collectors were considered traitors to the Jews because they were in league with the Romans. Many of them cheated the people by charging more than the necessary taxes and pocketing the difference. Being a tax collector, Matthew probably knew shorthand. When he recites Jesus, it is most likely word-for-word.

The record of Jesus calling him is found in Matthew 9:9-13, Mark 2:13-17, and Luke 5:27-28.

The theme of Matthew's Gospel is Jesus the Messiah. It is written to the Jews with the emphasis that the Messiah has come. Because of his shorthand skills, Matthew concentrated on what Jesus said.

His genealogy starts with Abraham and confirms the legal line of Jesus with his relation to King David. (Legally, the line follows the father and Joseph was the adopted father of Jesus.) His gospel is the only one that mentions the Magi's visit to the King.

The first miracle is the cleansing of a leper (represents sin) and ends with the Resurrection.

Mark

John Mark writes this gospel through the eyes of Peter. It is generally understood to be a collection of Peter's teachings. It is believed to be the oldest of the gospels, but the dating of the gospels is unproven. Archeological evidence points to earlier and earlier dates, but I will leave that for someone else to research. The emphasis of this journal is to learn more about The Christ and what He wanted us to know.

The calling of Peter can be found in Matthew 4:18-20, Mark 1:16-18, Luke 5:1-11. Mark writes of what Jesus did.

Matthew is writing to the Romans and emphasizes that Jesus is the Servant of God.

The first recorded miracle is the removal of the evil spirit from the man in the synagogue and ends with Jesus' Ascension.

Luke

The Gospel of Luke was written by a Gentile Physician name Luke. Luke traveled with Paul and was not an eye witness to the accounts written. He wrote in the highest form of Greek found in the New Testament and used many medical terms in this gospel. Sir William Ramsey set out to disprove Luke's gospel and discovered it was historically accurate and the most complete of all the gospels.

The theme of Luke's Gospel is Jesus the Son of Man. It is written to the Greeks with the emphasis that Jesus was a man—a perfect man—and focuses on how Jesus felt. It is the most narrative of the Gospels.

His genealogy starts with Joseph as the legal father of Jesus and the son-in-law of Heli. From there it goes through Mary's lineage—thus emphasizing the bloodline of the Christ—and ends with Adam.

The first miracle is also the removal of an evil spirit and ends with the promise of The Holy Spirit.Luke also wrote Acts.

John

Some say the Book of John is a good place to start when learning about Jesus, yet the depth of revelation is bottomless. This gospel has been described as shallow enough for a child to wake in, yet deep enough in which to wash an elephant.

The Gospel of John was written by a Jewish fisherman named John (not John the Baptist.) The record of Jesus calling him is found in Matthew 4:21-22, Mark 1:19-20, and Luke 5:7, 10.

The theme of John's Gospel is Jesus the Son of God. It is written to the church with the emphasis that Jesus is God. His genealogy, though not as recognizable as such, explains His preexistence (John 1:1-5). Jesus is the incarnate Word.

The first miracle is the wedding at Cana where Jesus turns water into wine and ends with the promise of His return.

John also wrote Revelation.

You may find yourself drawn to one gospel over another. Matthew illustrates Jesus as the Messiah and his security and power. Following the creator of the universe brings security. Mark reveals the suffering servant and shows the humbleness of Jesus. Repentance is encouraged. Luke describes the Son of Man. It is filled with forgiveness and understanding. John enforces that Jesus is the Son of God. It is transcendental and gives the reader a sense of escaping from this world into the world of Christ.

Whichever you are drawn toward, you need all four aspects of Jesus. Rely on His power. Be humbled by His servitude to mankind. Embrace forgiveness and understanding—both of Christ and our fellow man. But transcend the cruelty of this world and know on whom you rely.

The Gospels

	Matthew	Mark	Luke	John
Presents Jesus as	Messiah	Servant	Son of Man	Son of God
Genealogy	Abraham to Joseph- legal line	None	Mary to Adam – bloodline	Preexistent/Eternal
What Jesus	Said	Did	Felt	Was
Written to	Jews	Romans	Greeks	Church
1st Miracle	Cleanse a leper	Demon expelled	Demon expelled	Water to Wine
Ends with	Resurrection	Ascension	Promise of the Holy Spirit	Promise of Christ's return

How to Use This Journal

Use this book to fulfill your needs. Put in dates as you read, or don't. Give yourself date assignments, or don't. I only ask that you pray each day before reading and that you keep on reading until you finish both readings.

With the second reading, you will flip to many different books of The Bible. If you do not have tabs, you may want to buy some. I also use many bookmarks to keep places marked where I know I will return to shortly. One other hint: I put my finger where I am to begin reading and another finger where I am to stop. Otherwise, I have to keep referring to my list to see how far I am to read.

You will find space periodically and at the end of the book for you to journal. I recommend writing the date of your journaling and also acknowledging what day inspired your writing (e.g., Day 27).

"Do not think that I have come to abolish the Law or the Prophets; I have not come to abolish them but to fulfill them."

Matthew 5:17 NIV

The Book of Matthew

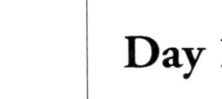 # Day 1

Date: _____

- o Matthew 3:15
- o Matthew 4:4
- o Matthew 4:7
- o Matthew 4:10
- o Matthew 4:17
- o Matthew 4:19
- o Matthew 5:3-48

To Whom is Jesus Speaking?
_____

Where is He?
_____

Time References?
_____

Notes/Verses/Thoughts:
_____
_____
_____
_____
_____
_____
_____
_____
_____
_____
_____
_____
_____
_____
_____
_____
_____
_____
_____
_____
_____

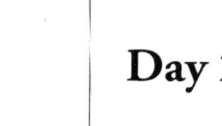

Day 2

Date: _____

- ○ Matthew 6:1-34
- ○ Matthew 7:1-27

To Whom is Jesus Speaking?
_____

Where is He?
_____

Time References?
_____

Notes/Verses/Thoughts:
_____
_____
_____
_____
_____
_____
_____
_____
_____
_____
_____
_____
_____
_____
_____
_____
_____
_____
_____
_____
_____
_____

Day 3

Date: _____

- ○ Matthew 8:3
- ○ Matthew 8:4
- ○ Matthew 8:7
- ○ Matthew 8:10-13
- ○ Matthew 8:20
- ○ Matthew 8:22
- ○ Matthew 8:26
- ○ Matthew 8:32
- ○ Matthew 9:2
- ○ Matthew 9:4-6
- ○ Matthew 9:9
- ○ Matthew 9:12
- ○ Matthew 9:13
- ○ Matthew 9:15-17
- ○ Matthew 9:22
- ○ Matthew 9:24
- ○ Matthew 9:28
- ○ Matthew 9:29
- ○ Matthew 9:30
- ○ Matthew 9:37
- ○ Matthew 10:5-42

To Whom is Jesus Speaking?
_____

Where is He?
_____

Time References?
_____

Notes/Verses/Thoughts:

Day 4

Date: _____

- Matthew 11:4-19
- Matthew 11:21-30
- Matthew 12:5-8
- Matthew 12:11-12
- Matthew 12:13
- Matthew 12:25-37
- Matthew 12:39-45
- Matthew 12:48
- Matthew 12:49
- Matthew 12:50

To Whom is Jesus Speaking?
_____

Where is He?
_____

Time References?
_____

Notes/Verses/Thoughts:
_____
_____
_____
_____
_____
_____
_____
_____
_____
_____
_____
_____
_____
_____
_____
_____
_____
_____
_____
_____
_____
_____
_____
_____

The Messiah

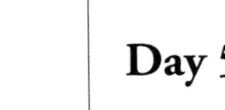

Day 5

Date: _____

- Matthew 13:3-9
- Matthew 13:11-23
- Matthew 13:24-30
- Matthew 13:31-32
- Matthew 13:33
- Matthew 13:37-51
- Matthew 13:52
- Matthew 13:57

To Whom is Jesus Speaking?
_____

Where is He?
_____

Time References?
_____

Notes/Verses/Thoughts:
_____
_____
_____
_____
_____
_____
_____
_____
_____
_____
_____
_____
_____
_____
_____
_____
_____
_____
_____
_____
_____

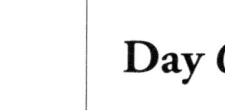

Day 6

Date: _____

- Matthew 14:16
- Matthew 14:18
- Matthew 14:27
- Matthew 14:29
- Matthew 14:31
- Matthew 15:3-9
- Matthew 15:10-11
- Matthew 15:13-14
- Matthew 15:16-20
- Matthew 15:24
- Matthew 15:26
- Matthew 15:28
- Matthew 15:32
- Matthew 15:34
- Matthew 16:2-4
- Matthew 16:6
- Matthew 16:8-11
- Matthew 16:13
- Matthew 16:15
- Matthew 16:17-19
- Matthew 16:23
- Matthew 16:24-28

To Whom is Jesus Speaking?
_____

Where is He?
_____

Time References?
_____

Notes/Verses/Thoughts:
_____
_____
_____
_____
_____
_____
_____
_____
_____
_____
_____
_____
_____
_____
_____
_____
_____
_____
_____
_____
_____
_____

The Messiah

Day 7

Date: _____

- ○ Matthew 17:7
- ○ Matthew 17:9
- ○ Matthew 17:11-12
- ○ Matthew 17:17
- ○ Matthew 17:20-21
- ○ Matthew 17:22-23
- ○ Matthew 17:25
- ○ Matthew 17:26
- ○ Matthew 17:27
- ○ Matthew 18:3-9
- ○ Matthew 18:10-14
- ○ Matthew 18:15-20
- ○ Matthew 18:23-35

To Whom is Jesus Speaking?
_____

Where is He?
_____

Time References?
_____

Notes/Verses/Thoughts:
_____
_____
_____
_____
_____
_____
_____
_____
_____
_____
_____
_____
_____
_____
_____
_____
_____
_____
_____
_____
_____
_____

Day 8

Date: _____

- ○ Matthew 19:4-6
- ○ Matthew 19:8-9
- ○ Matthew 19:11-12
- ○ Matthew 19:14
- ○ Matthew 19:17
- ○ Matthew 19:18-19
- ○ Matthew 19:21
- ○ Matthew 19:23-24
- ○ Matthew 19:26
- ○ Matthew 19:28-30
- ○ Matthew 20:1-16
- ○ Matthew 20:18-19
- ○ Matthew 20:21
- ○ Matthew 20:22
- ○ Matthew 20:23
- ○ Matthew 20:25-28
- ○ Matthew 20:32

To Whom is Jesus Speaking?
_____

Where is He?
_____

Time References?
_____

Notes/Verses/Thoughts:
_____
_____
_____
_____
_____
_____
_____
_____
_____
_____
_____
_____
_____
_____
_____
_____
_____
_____
_____
_____
_____
_____
_____
_____
_____
_____

The Messiah

Day 9

Date: _____

- ○ Matthew 21:2-3
- ○ Matthew 21:13
- ○ Matthew 21:16
- ○ Matthew 21:19
- ○ Matthew 21:21-22
- ○ Matthew 21:24-25
- ○ Matthew 21:27
- ○ Matthew 21:28-40
- ○ Matthew 21:42-44
- ○ Matthew 22:2-14
- ○ Matthew 22:18-19
- ○ Matthew 22:20
- ○ Matthew 22:21
- ○ Matthew 22:29-32
- ○ Matthew 22:37-40
- ○ Matthew 22:42
- ○ Matthew 22:43-45

To Whom is Jesus Speaking? _____

Where is He? _____

Time References? _____

Notes/Verses/Thoughts:
_____

The Messiah

Day 10

Date: _____

- Matthew 23:2-39

To Whom is Jesus Speaking?
_____

Where is He?
_____

Time References?
_____

Notes/Verses/Thoughts:
_____
_____
_____
_____
_____
_____
_____
_____
_____
_____
_____
_____
_____
_____
_____
_____
_____
_____
_____
_____
_____
_____
_____

Day 11

Date: _____

- o Matthew 24:2
- o Matthew 24:4-51

To Whom is Jesus Speaking?
_____

Where is He?
_____

Time References?
_____

Notes/Verses/Thoughts:
_____
_____
_____
_____
_____
_____
_____
_____
_____
_____
_____
_____
_____
_____
_____
_____
_____
_____
_____
_____
_____
_____
_____
_____
_____

Day 12

Date: _____

- Matthew 25:1-46

To Whom is Jesus Speaking?
_____

Where is He?
_____

Time References?
_____

Notes/Verses/Thoughts:
_____
_____
_____
_____
_____
_____
_____
_____
_____
_____
_____
_____
_____
_____
_____
_____
_____
_____
_____
_____
_____
_____
_____

The Messiah

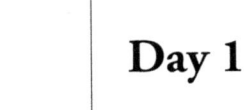

Day 13

Date: _____

- ○ Matthew 26:2
- ○ Matthew 26:10-13
- ○ Matthew 26:18
- ○ Matthew 26:21
- ○ Matthew 26:23-24
- ○ Matthew 26:25
- ○ Matthew 26:26
- ○ Matthew 26:27-29
- ○ Matthew 26:31-32
- ○ Matthew 26:34
- ○ Matthew 26:36
- ○ Matthew 26:38
- ○ Matthew 26:39
- ○ Matthew 26:40
- ○ Matthew 26:41
- ○ Matthew 26:42
- ○ Matthew 26:45-46
- ○ Matthew 26:50
- ○ Matthew 26:52-54
- ○ Matthew 26-55-56
- ○ Matthew 26:64
- ○ Matthew 26:75
- ○ Matthew 27:11
- ○ Matthew 27:46
- ○ Matthew 28:9
- ○ Matthew 28:10
- ○ Matthew 28:18-20

To Whom is Jesus Speaking?
_____

Where is He?
_____

Time References?
_____

Notes/Verses/Thoughts:
_____
_____
_____
_____
_____
_____
_____
_____
_____
_____
_____
_____
_____
_____
_____
_____
_____
_____
_____
_____
_____

You have gained knowledge, but have you gained wisdom? Knowledge is learning facts. Wisdom is applying them. What have you learned? How can you apply it?

"See, my servant will act wisely; he will be raised and lifted up and highly
exalted. Just as there were many who were appalled at him
—his appearance was so disfigured beyond that of any human
being and his form marred beyond human likeness—
so he will sprinkle many nations, and kings will shut their mouths
because of him. For what they were not told, they will see,
and what they have not heard, they will understand."

Isaiah 52:13-15 NIV

The Book of Mark

Day 14

Date: _____

- ○ Mark 1:15
- ○ Mark 1:17
- ○ Mark 1:25
- ○ Mark 1:38
- ○ Mark 1:41
- ○ Mark 1:44
- ○ Mark 2:5
- ○ Mark 2:8-11
- ○ Mark 2:14
- ○ Mark 2:17
- ○ Mark 2:19-22
- ○ Mark 2:25-27
- ○ Mark 3:3
- ○ Mark 3:4
- ○ Mark 3:5
- ○ Mark 3:23-29
- ○ Mark 3:33-35
- ○ Mark 4:3-9
- ○ Mark 4:11-20
- ○ Mark 4:21-25
- ○ Mark 4:26-29
- ○ Mark 4:30-32
- ○ Mark 4:35
- ○ Mark 4:39
- ○ Mark 4:40

To Whom is Jesus Speaking?
_____

Where is He?
_____

Time References?
_____

Notes/Verses/Thoughts:
_____
_____
_____
_____
_____
_____
_____
_____
_____
_____
_____
_____
_____
_____
_____
_____
_____
_____
_____
_____
_____
_____
_____
_____

Day 15

Date: _____

- Mark 5:8
- Mark 5:19
- Mark 5:30
- Mark 5:31
- Mark 5:34
- Mark 5:36
- Mark 5:39
- Mark 5:41
- Mark 6:4
- Mark 6:8-11
- Mark 6:31
- Mark 6:37
- Mark 6:38
- Mark 6:50
- Mark 7:6-23
- Mark 7:27
- Mark 7:29
- Mark 7:34
- Mark 8:2-3
- Mark 8:5
- Mark 8:12
- Mark 8:15
- Mark 8:17-32
- Mark 8:23
- Mark 8:26
- Mark 8:27
- Mark 8:29
- Mark 8:33-38

To Whom is Jesus Speaking?
_____

Where is He?
_____

Time References?
_____

Notes/Verses/Thoughts:
_____
_____
_____
_____
_____
_____
_____
_____
_____
_____
_____
_____
_____
_____
_____
_____
_____
_____
_____
_____
_____
_____
_____

Day 16

Date: _____

- ○ Mark 9:1
- ○ Mark 9:12-13
- ○ Mark 9:16
- ○ Mark 9:19
- ○ Mark 9:21
- ○ Mark 9:23
- ○ Mark 9:25
- ○ Mark 9:29
- ○ Mark 9:31
- ○ Mark 9:33
- ○ Mark 9:35
- ○ Mark 9:37
- ○ Mark 9:39-50
- ○ Mark 10:3
- ○ Mark 10:5-9
- ○ Mark 10:11-12
- ○ Mark 10:14-15
- ○ Mark 10:18-19
- ○ Mark 10:21
- ○ Mark 10:23-25
- ○ Mark 10:27
- ○ Mark 10:29-31
- ○ Mark 10:33-34
- ○ Mark 10:36
- ○ Mark 10:38
- ○ Mark 10:39-40
- ○ Mark 10:42-45
- ○ Mark 10:49
- ○ Mark 10:51-52

To Whom is Jesus Speaking?
_____

Where is He?
_____

Time References?
_____

Notes/Verses/Thoughts:
_____
_____
_____
_____
_____
_____
_____
_____
_____
_____
_____
_____
_____
_____
_____
_____
_____
_____
_____
_____
_____
_____
_____
_____

Day 17

Date: _____

- ○ Mark 11:2-3
- ○ Mark 11:14
- ○ Mark 11:17
- ○ Mark 11:22-26
- ○ Mark 11:29-30
- ○ Mark 11:33
- ○ Mark 12:1-11
- ○ Mark 12:15-17
- ○ Mark 12:24-27
- ○ Mark 12:29-31
- ○ Mark 12:34
- ○ Mark 12:35-40
- ○ Mark 12:43-44

To Whom is Jesus Speaking? _____

Where is He? _____

Time References? _____

Notes/Verses/Thoughts:
_____
_____
_____
_____
_____
_____
_____
_____
_____
_____
_____
_____
_____
_____
_____
_____
_____
_____
_____
_____
_____
_____

The Suffering Servant

Day 18

Date: _____

- ○ Mark 13:2
- ○ Mark 13:5-37
- ○ Mark 14:6-9
- ○ Mark 14:13-15
- ○ Mark 14:18
- ○ Mark 14:20-21
- ○ Mark 14:22
- ○ Mark 14:24-25
- ○ Mark 14:27-28
- ○ Mark 14:30
- ○ Mark 14:32
- ○ Mark 14:34
- ○ Mark 14:36-38
- ○ Mark 14:41-42
- ○ Mark 14:48-49
- ○ Mark 14:62
- ○ Mark 14:72
- ○ Mark 15:2
- ○ Mark 15:34
- ○ Mark 16:15-18

To Whom is Jesus Speaking?
_____

Where is He?
_____

Time References?
_____

Notes/Verses/Thoughts:
_____
_____
_____
_____
_____
_____
_____
_____
_____
_____
_____
_____
_____
_____
_____
_____
_____
_____
_____
_____
_____
_____

The Suffering Servant

What new knowledge have you gained? How can you apply it?

"Let your hand rest on the man at your right hand,
the son of man you have raised up for yourself."

Psalm 80:17

The Book of Luke

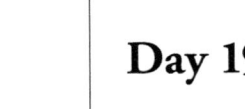

Day 19

Date: _____

- ○ Luke 2:49
- ○ Luke 4:4
- ○ Luke 4:8
- ○ Luke 4:12
- ○ Luke 4:18-19
- ○ Luke 4:21
- ○ Luke 4:23-27
- ○ Luke 4:35
- ○ Luke 4:43
- ○ Luke 5:4
- ○ Luke 5:10
- ○ Luke 5:13-14
- ○ Luke 5:20
- ○ Luke 5:22-24
- ○ Luke 5:27
- ○ Luke 5:31-32
- ○ Luke 5:34-39
- ○ Luke 6:3-5
- ○ Luke 6:8-10
- ○ Luke 6:20-26
- ○ Luke 6:27-36
- ○ Luke 6:37-42
- ○ Luke 6:43-45
- ○ Luke 6:46-49

To Whom is Jesus Speaking? _____

Where is He? _____

Time References? _____

Notes/Verses/Thoughts:
_____
_____
_____
_____
_____
_____
_____
_____
_____
_____
_____
_____
_____
_____
_____
_____
_____
_____
_____
_____
_____
_____
_____

The Son of Man

Day 20

Date: _____

- ○ Luke 7:9
- ○ Luke 7:13-14
- ○ Luke 7:22-28
- ○ Luke 7:31-35
- ○ Luke 7:40-48
- ○ Luke 7:50
- ○ Luke 8:5-8
- ○ Luke 8:10-15
- ○ Luke 8:16-18
- ○ Luke 8:21
- ○ Luke 8:22
- ○ Luke 8:25
- ○ Luke 8:30
- ○ Luke 8:39
- ○ Luke 8:45-46
- ○ Luke 8:48
- ○ Luke 8:50
- ○ Luke 8:52
- ○ Luke 8:54

To Whom is Jesus Speaking? _____

Where is He? _____

Time References? _____

Notes/Verses/Thoughts:
_____

Day 21

Date: _____

- Luke 9:3-5
- Luke 9:13-14
- Luke 9:18
- Luke 9:20
- Luke 9:22-27
- Luke 9:41
- Luke 9:44
- Luke 9:48
- Luke 9:50
- Luke 9:58-60
- Luke 9:62
- Luke 10:2-16
- Luke 10:18-24
- Luke 10:26
- Luke 10:28
- Luke 10:30-37
- Luke 10:41-42

To Whom is Jesus Speaking? _____

Where is He? _____

Time References? _____

Notes/Verses/Thoughts:

Day 22

Date: _____

- Luke 11:2-13
- Luke 11:17-26
- Luke 11:28
- Luke 11:29-32
- Luke 11:33-36
- Luke 11:39-44
- Luke 11:46-52

To Whom is Jesus Speaking?
_____

Where is He?
_____

Time References?
_____

Notes/Verses/Thoughts:
_____
_____
_____
_____
_____
_____
_____
_____
_____
_____
_____
_____
_____
_____
_____
_____
_____
_____
_____
_____
_____
_____
_____
_____
_____

Day 23

Date: _____

- ○ Luke 12:1-12
- ○ Luke 12:14-21
- ○ Luke 12:22-34
- ○ Luke 12:35-48
- ○ Luke 12:49-53
- ○ Luke 12:54-59

To Whom is Jesus Speaking?
_____

Where is He?
_____

Time References?
_____

Notes/Verses/Thoughts:
_____
_____
_____
_____
_____
_____
_____
_____
_____
_____
_____
_____
_____
_____
_____
_____
_____
_____
_____
_____
_____
_____
_____
_____

Day 24

Date: _____

- ○ Luke 13:2-9
- ○ Luke 13:12
- ○ Luke 13:15-16
- ○ Luke 13:18-21
- ○ Luke 13:24-30
- ○ Luke 13:32-35

To Whom is Jesus Speaking?
_____

Where is He?
_____

Time References?
_____

Notes/Verses/Thoughts:
_____
_____
_____
_____
_____
_____
_____
_____
_____
_____
_____
_____
_____
_____
_____
_____
_____
_____
_____
_____
_____
_____
_____
_____
_____

Day 25

Date: _____

- ○ Luke 14:3
- ○ Luke 14:5
- ○ Luke 14:8-14
- ○ Luke 14:16-24
- ○ Luke 14:26-35
- ○ Luke 15:4-7
- ○ Luke 15:8-10
- ○ Luke 15:11-32

To Whom is Jesus Speaking?
_____

Where is He?
_____

Time References?
_____

Notes/Verses/Thoughts:
_____
_____
_____
_____
_____
_____
_____
_____
_____
_____
_____
_____
_____
_____
_____
_____
_____
_____
_____
_____
_____
_____
_____

Day 26

Date: _____

- ○ Luke 16:1-15
- ○ Luke 16:16-18
- ○ Luke 16:19-31
- ○ Luke 17:1-4
- ○ Luke 17:6-10
- ○ Luke 17:14
- ○ Luke 17:17-19
- ○ Luke 17:20-37

To Whom is Jesus Speaking?
_____

Where is He?
_____

Time References?
_____

Notes/Verses/Thoughts:
_____

☐ **Day 27**

Date: _____

- ○ Luke 18:2-8
- ○ Luke 18:10-14
- ○ Luke 18:16-17
- ○ Luke 18:19-20
- ○ Luke 18:22
- ○ Luke 18:24-25
- ○ Luke 18:27
- ○ Luke 18:29-30
- ○ Luke 18:31-33
- ○ Luke 18:41-42
- ○ Luke 19:5
- ○ Luke 19:9-10
- ○ Luke 19:12-27
- ○ Luke 19:30-31
- ○ Luke 19:40
- ○ Luke 19:42-44
- ○ Luke 19:46

To Whom is Jesus Speaking?
_____
Where is He?
_____
Time References?
_____
Notes/Verses/Thoughts:
_____
_____
_____
_____
_____
_____
_____
_____
_____
_____
_____
_____
_____
_____
_____
_____
_____
_____
_____
_____
_____
_____
_____
_____

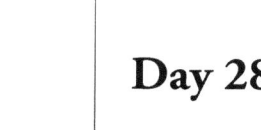

Day 28

Date: _____

- Luke 20:3
- Luke 20:8
- Luke 20:9-18
- Luke 20:24-25
- Luke 20:34-38
- Luke 20:41-44
- Luke 20:46-47
- Luke 21:3-4
- Luke 21:8-36

To Whom is Jesus Speaking?
_____

Where is He?
_____

Time References?
_____

Notes/Verses/Thoughts:
_____
_____
_____
_____
_____
_____
_____
_____
_____
_____
_____
_____
_____
_____
_____
_____
_____
_____
_____
_____
_____
_____
_____
_____

Day 29

Date: _____

- o Luke 22:8-12
- o Luke 22:15-22
- o Luke 22:25-38
- o Luke 22:40
- o Luke 22:42
- o Luke 22:46
- o Luke 22:48
- o Luke 22:51
- o Luke 22:52-53
- o Luke 22:61
- o Luke 22:67-69
- o Luke 22:70
- o Luke 23:3
- o Luke 23:28-31
- o Luke 23:34
- o Luke 23:43
- o Luke 23:46
- o Luke 24:7
- o Luke 24:17
- o Luke 24:19
- o Luke 24:25-26
- o Luke 24:36-39
- o Luke 24:41
- o Luke 24:44
- o Luke 24:46-49

To Whom is Jesus Speaking?
_____

Where is He?
_____

Time References?
_____

Notes/Verses/Thoughts:

Any surprises? Are you allowing Jesus to teach you? Allow the Holy Spirit to guide you.

"And I will pour out on the house of David
and the inhabitants of Jerusalem
a spirit of grace and supplication.
They will look on me, the one they have pierced,
and they will mourn for him as one mourns for an only child,
and grieve bitterly for him as one grieves for a firstborn son."

Zechariah 12:10 NIV

The Book of John

Day 30

Date: _____

- ○ John 1:37
- ○ John 1:39
- ○ John 1:42
- ○ John 1:43
- ○ John 1:47
- ○ John 1:48
- ○ John 1:50-51
- ○ John 2:4
- ○ John 2:7-8
- ○ John 2:16
- ○ John 2:19
- ○ John 3:3
- ○ John 3:5-8
- ○ John 3:10-21

To Whom is Jesus Speaking?
_____

Where is He?
_____

Time References?
_____

Notes/Verses/Thoughts:
_____
_____
_____
_____
_____
_____
_____
_____
_____
_____
_____
_____
_____
_____
_____
_____
_____
_____
_____
_____
_____
_____

Day 31

Date: _____

- John 4:7
- John 4:10
- John 4:13-14
- John 4:16-18
- John 4:21-24
- John 4:26
- John 4:32
- John 4:34-38
- John 4:48
- John 4:50
- John 4:53
- John 5:6
- John 5:8
- John 5:11
- John 5:14
- John 5:17
- John 5:19-30
- John 5:31-47

To Whom is Jesus Speaking? _____

Where is He? _____

Time References? _____

Notes/Verses/Thoughts:
_____

The Great I Am

Day 32

Date: _____

- o John 6:5
- o John 6:10
- o John 6:12
- o John 6:20
- o John 6:26-27
- o John 6:29
- o John 6:32-33
- o John 6:35-51
- o John 6:53-58
- o John 6:61-64
- o John 6:65
- o John 6:67
- o John 6:70
- o John 7:6-8
- o John 7:16-19
- o John 7:21-24
- o John 7:28-29
- o John 7:33-34
- o John 7:36-38

To Whom is Jesus Speaking?
_____

Where is He?
_____

Time References?
_____

Notes/Verses/Thoughts:
_____
_____
_____
_____
_____
_____
_____
_____
_____
_____
_____
_____
_____
_____
_____
_____
_____
_____
_____
_____
_____
_____
_____
_____

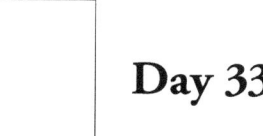

Day 33

Date: _____

- ○ John 8:7
- ○ John 8:10-11
- ○ John 8:12
- ○ John 8:14-19
- ○ John 8:21-26
- ○ John 8:28-29
- ○ John 8:31-32
- ○ John 8:34-41
- ○ John 8:42-47
- ○ John 8:49-51
- ○ John 8:54-56
- ○ John 8:58
- ○ John 9:3-5
- ○ John 9:7
- ○ John 9:35
- ○ John 9:37
- ○ John 9:39
- ○ John 9:41

To Whom is Jesus Speaking?
_____

Where is He?
_____

Time References?
_____

Notes/Verses/Thoughts:
_____

The Great I Am

Day 34

Date: _____

- ○ John 10:1-5
- ○ John 10:7-18
- ○ John 10:25-30
- ○ John 10:32
- ○ John 10:34-38
- ○ John 11:4
- ○ John 11:7
- ○ John 11:9-11
- ○ John 11:14-15
- ○ John 11:23
- ○ John 11:25-26
- ○ John 11:34
- ○ John 11:39
- ○ John 11:40-44

To Whom is Jesus Speaking?
_____

Where is He?
_____

Time References?
_____

Notes/Verses/Thoughts:
_____
_____
_____
_____
_____
_____
_____
_____
_____
_____
_____
_____
_____
_____
_____
_____
_____
_____
_____
_____
_____
_____

The Great I Am

Day 35

Date: _____

- John 12:7-9
- John 12:23-28
- John 12:30-32
- John 12:34-36
- John 12:44-50
- John 13:7-8
- John 13:10
- John 13:12-21
- John 13:26-27
- John 13:31-35
- John 13:36
- John 13:38

To Whom is Jesus Speaking?
_____

Where is He?
_____

Time References?
_____

Notes/Verses/Thoughts:
_____
_____
_____
_____
_____
_____
_____
_____
_____
_____
_____
_____
_____
_____
_____
_____
_____
_____
_____
_____
_____
_____

The Great I Am

Day 36

Date: _____

- John 14:1-4
- John 14:6-7
- John 14:9-14
- John 14:15-21
- John 14:23-31
- John 15:1-17
- John 15:18-27

To Whom is Jesus Speaking?
_____

Where is He?
_____

Time References?
_____

Notes/Verses/Thoughts:
_____
_____
_____
_____
_____
_____
_____
_____
_____
_____
_____
_____
_____
_____
_____
_____
_____
_____
_____
_____
_____
_____
_____

Day 37

Date: _____

- ○ John 16:1-4
- ○ John 16:5-16
- ○ John 16:17-28
- ○ John 16:31-33
- ○ John 17:1-5
- ○ John 17:6-19
- ○ John 17:20-26

To Whom is Jesus Speaking?
_____

Where is He?
_____

Time References?
_____

Notes/Verses/Thoughts:
_____
_____
_____
_____
_____
_____
_____
_____
_____
_____
_____
_____
_____
_____
_____
_____
_____
_____
_____
_____
_____
_____
_____
_____

The Great I Am

Day 38

Date: _____

- John 18:4
- John 18:5
- John 18:6
- John 18:7
- John 18:8
- John 18:9
- John 18:11
- John 18:20-21
- John 18:23
- John 18:34
- John 18:36-37
- John 19:11
- John 19:26-27
- John 19:28
- John 19:30
- John 20:15
- John 20:16
- John 20:17
- John 20:19
- John 20:21
- John 20:22-23
- John 20:26-27
- John 20:29
- John 21:5-6
- John 21:10
- John 21:12
- John 21:15-19
- John 21:22
- John 21:23

To Whom is Jesus Speaking? _____

Where is He? _____

Time References? _____

Notes/Verses/Thoughts:
_____
_____
_____
_____
_____
_____
_____
_____
_____
_____
_____
_____
_____
_____
_____
_____
_____
_____
_____
_____
_____
_____
_____

Do you see the different perspectives of the four Gospels? Which reached you the best and why?

"So what shall I do? I will pray with my spirit,
but I will also pray with my understanding;
I will sing with my spirit,
but I will also sing with my understanding."

1 Corinthians 14:15

Acts,
1 Corinthians,
2 Corinthians,
Revelation

Day 39

Date: _____

- ○ Acts 1:4-5
- ○ Acts 1:7-8
- ○ Acts 9:4-6
- ○ Acts 9:10-12
- ○ Acts 9:15-16
- ○ Acts 10:13
- ○ Acts 10:15
- ○ Acts 11:7
- ○ Acts 11:9
- ○ Acts 11:16
- ○ Acts 18:9-10
- ○ Acts 20:35
- ○ Acts 22:7-8
- ○ Acts 22:10
- ○ Acts 22:18
- ○ Acts 22:21
- ○ Acts 23:11
- ○ Acts 26:14-18
- ○ 1 Corinthians 11:24-25
- ○ 2 Corinthians 12:9

To Whom is Jesus Speaking?
_____

Where is He?
_____

Time References?
_____

Notes/Verses/Thoughts:
_____
_____
_____
_____
_____
_____
_____
_____
_____
_____
_____
_____
_____
_____
_____
_____
_____
_____
_____
_____
_____
_____
_____
_____

Day 40

Date: _____

- o   Revelations 1:8
- o   Revelations 1:11
- o   Revelations 1:17-20
- o   Revelations 2:1-7
- o   Revelations 2:8-11
- o   Revelations 2:12-17
- o   Revelations 2:18-29
- o   Revelations 3:1-6
- o   Revelations 3:7-13
- o   Revelations 3:14-22
- o   Revelations 4:1
- o   Revelations 16:15
- o   Revelations 22:7
- o   Revelations 22:12-16
- o   Revelations 22:20

To Whom is Jesus Speaking?
_____

Where is He?
_____

Time References?
_____

Notes/Verses/Thoughts:
_____
_____
_____
_____
_____
_____
_____
_____
_____
_____
_____
_____
_____
_____
_____
_____
_____
_____
_____
_____
_____
_____
_____

Reflections

Second Reading with Old Testament References

If we think of our beliefs as a clock, with twelve as our current understanding, when we learn, we often pull away from noon and head toward three. We become uneasy and want to revert back to noon—back to our comfort zone. Some will. The brave will continue.

More insight is gained as we journey toward six. Confusion and anxiety grow. Something's wrong. Is it our past or current understanding? Hatred may creep in because we feel foolish or deceived. The temptation to ignore this new view grows, but we must not succumb. On the other hand, some stay in this half-truth understanding and rebuff their old beliefs. We must not do that. We must keep learning because we find as we keep exploring, we start heading back toward noon via nine o'clock. When we return to noon, we have a greater, deeper, more insightful view. We discover we weren't totally wrong (like six o'clock felt) but rather we had relied on a limited understanding.

The big question is: which is correct? Our noon or six o'clock beliefs? What if we were stuck at six and our eyes have been opened to noon?

The great decoder ring is this: are we heading toward love and understanding? Did we find a greater sense of peace or an increase in agitation? We must pray and ask God for wisdom. We must ask the Holy Spirit to whisper in our ear. We must continually seek understanding on the path of love. God does not fill our hearts with hatred and fear. If that is where we find ourselves, we stand at six. Keep reading scripture. Keep praying. It's a long journey; it takes a lifetime.

Take your time on this next forty-day reading. Gain greater insight from Jesus's words. Do not worry if you pull away from noon. Keep praying and follow the path of deeper love, greater truth. Learn the gospel.

"The New Testament is in the Old Testament concealed and the Old Testament is in the New Testament revealed."

- Dr. Chuck Missler

The Book of Matthew

For the Book of Matthew, I reference the Old Testament **prior** to the verse it is to illuminate. Since the Gospel is written to the Jew and for the Jew, I thought it appropriate to start with what they knew prior to the arrival of Jesus.

Having most of us grown up with a belief in Jesus, we forget that Jesus was sent to teach God's chosen people and was, in fact, a Jew. The Old Testament is filled with prophecies of the rejection of The Messiah, but many Jews followed Christ and died for their belief. We take for granted the gift of God's Grace without realizing the difficulty that decision is for many.

Persecution of Christians is prevalent throughout the world, but particularly in Communist and Islamic Governments. Pray for your fellow believers and contemplate the risk they take to follow Christ.

If you live without fear of voicing your Christianity, do not take that for granted. Let your belief in Jesus The Messiah be known. Openly living your faith is a privilege many do not have.

Over the next forty days, learn more about Our Savior for which many have died—including most of the Gospel writers. It is believed that of the twelve disciples, only John died a natural death.

Day 1

Date: _____

- ○ Matthew 3:15
- ○ Matthew 4:4
- ○ Exodus 17:1-7
- ○ Matthew 4:7
- ○ Deuteronomy 6:13-16
- ○ Matthew 4:10
- ○ Isaiah 56:1-2
- ○ Matthew 4:17
- ○ Matthew 4:19
- ○ Psalm 37:1-34
- ○ Matthew 5:3-5
- ○ Isaiah 55
- ○ Matthew 5:6
- ○ Psalm 41:1-2
- ○ Matthew 5:7
- ○ Psalm 24:1-6
- ○ Matthew 5:8
- ○ Isaiah 32:17
- ○ Matthew 5:9
- ○ Isaiah 51:11-16
- ○ Matthew 5:10-12
- ○ Isaiah 40:6-9
- ○ Matthew 5:13-26
- ○ Proverbs 6:20-33
- ○ Matthew 5:27-30
- ○ Deuteronomy 24:1
- ○ Matthew 5:31-32
- ○ Deuteronomy 23:21-23
- ○ Ecclesiastes 5:4-6
- ○ Matthew 5:33-37

To Whom is Jesus Speaking?
_____

Where is He?
_____

Time References?
_____

Notes/Verses/Thoughts:
_____
_____
_____
_____
_____
_____
_____
_____
_____
_____
_____
_____
_____
_____
_____
_____
_____
_____
_____
_____
_____
_____
_____
_____

Day 2

Date: _____

- ○ Leviticus 24:17-22
- ○ Deuteronomy 19:15-21
- ○ Matthew 5:38-42
- ○ Leviticus 19:18
- ○ Psalm 139:19-24
- ○ Matthew 5:43-48
- ○ Matthew 6:1-4
- ○ Ecclesiastes 5:2-3
- ○ Ecclesiastes 5: 7
- ○ Matthew 6:5-8
- ○ Jeremiah 3:12-19
- ○ Matthew 6:9-10
- ○ Proverbs 30:7-9
- ○ Matthew 6:11-15
- ○ Isaiah 58:1-9a
- ○ Zechariah 7:5
- ○ Zechariah 8:19
- ○ Matthew 6:16-18
- ○ Proverbs 23:4-5
- ○ Matthew 6:19-24
- ○ Psalm 145:8-21
- ○ Matthew 6:25-34
- ○ Ezekiel 35:11
- ○ Matthew 7:1-5
- ○ Jeremiah 15:19
- ○ Matthew 7:6

To Whom is Jesus Speaking?
_____

Where is He?
_____

Time References?
_____

Notes/Verses/Thoughts:
_____
_____
_____
_____
_____
_____
_____
_____
_____
_____
_____
_____
_____
_____
_____
_____
_____
_____
_____
_____
_____
_____
_____
_____

The Messiah

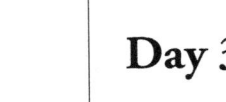

Day 3

Date: _____

- ○ Proverbs 8:12-31
- ○ Psalm 10:1-4
- ○ Jeremiah 29:11-14
- ○ Matthew 7:7-12
- ○ Proverbs 1:1-7
- ○ Matthew 7:13-14
- ○ Jeremiah 23:16-29
- ○ Matthew 7:15-20
- ○ Hosea 8:1-5
- ○ Psalm 91:14-16
- ○ Matthew 7:21-27
- ○ Leviticus 14:1-7
- ○ Matthew 8:3-4
- ○ Psalm 107:19-22
- ○ Matthew 8:7
- ○ Isaiah 59:19-21
- ○ Matthew 8:10-13
- ○ Matthew 8:20
- ○ Matthew 8:22
- ○ Psalm 89:9
- ○ Matthew 8:26
- ○ Matthew 8:32

To Whom is Jesus Speaking? _____

Where is He? _____

Time References? _____

Notes/Verses/Thoughts:
_____
_____
_____
_____
_____
_____
_____
_____
_____
_____
_____
_____
_____
_____
_____
_____
_____
_____
_____
_____
_____
_____
_____
_____

The Messiah

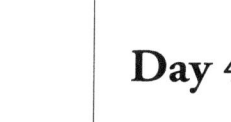

Day 4

Date: _____

- ○ Matthew 9:2
- ○ Matthew 9:4-6
- ○ Matthew 9:9
- ○ Hosea 6:1-6
- ○ Matthew 9:12
- ○ Matthew 9:13
- ○ Matthew 9:15-17
- ○ Matthew 9:22
- ○ Matthew 9:24
- ○ Matthew 9:28
- ○ Matthew 9:29
- ○ Matthew 9:30
- ○ Matthew 9:37
- ○ Jeremiah 50:6
- ○ Matthew 10:5-11
- ○ 1 Samuel 25:5-6
- ○ Matthew 10:12-16
- ○ Isaiah 8:11-13
- ○ Matthew 10:17-33
- ○ Micah 7:4-7
- ○ Matthew 10:34-41
- ○ Proverb 19:17
- ○ Matthew 10:42
- ○ Matthew 11:4-9
- ○ Malachi 3:1
- ○ Matthew 11:10-13
- ○ Malachi 4:5-6

To Whom is Jesus Speaking? _____

Where is He? _____

Time References? _____

Notes/Verses/Thoughts:
_____
_____
_____
_____
_____
_____
_____
_____
_____
_____
_____
_____
_____
_____
_____
_____
_____
_____
_____
_____
_____

(Continued)

- Matthew 11:14-19
- Matthew 11:21
- Amos 1:9-10
- Matthew 11:22-27
- Exodus 33:13-14
- Matthew 11:28-30

Notes/Verses/Thoughts:

Day 5

Date: _____

- Matthew 12:3
- 1 Samuel 21:1-6
- Matthew 12:4
- Leviticus 24:5-9
- Matthew 12:5-8
- 1 Chronicles 16:8-36
- Matthew 12:11-12
- Matthew 12:13
- Matthew 12:25-34
- Proverbs 12:13-23
- Matthew 12:35-37
- Matthew 12:39
- Jonah 1:17
- Matthew 12:40-41
- Jonah 1:2
- Jonah 3:5
- Matthew 12:42
- 2 Chronicles 9:1-8
- Matthew 12:43-45
- Psalm 78:1-8
- Matthew 12:48
- Matthew 12:49
- Matthew 12:50

To Whom is Jesus Speaking?
_____

Where is He?
_____

Time References?
_____

Notes/Verses/Thoughts:
_____

The Messiah

Day 6

Date: _____

- Matthew 13:3
- Jeremiah 6:10
- Matthew 13:4-9
- Deuteronomy 29:2-15
- Matthew 13:11-12
- Ezekiel 12:1-2
- Matthew 13:13
- Isaiah 6:8-10
- Matthew 13:14-18
- Matthew 13:19-23
- Jeremiah 5:26-28
- Matthew 13:24-31
- Ezekiel 31:1-14
- Matthew 13:32-33
- Exodus 12:6-8
- Ezekiel 17:22-24
- Joel 3:13
- Matthew 13:37-51
- Matthew 13:52
- Matthew 13:57
- 2 Kings 4:1-7
- Matthew 14:16
- Matthew 14:18
- Matthew 14:27
- Matthew 14:29
- Matthew 14:31

To Whom is Jesus Speaking? _____

Where is He? _____

Time References? _____

Notes/Verses/Thoughts:

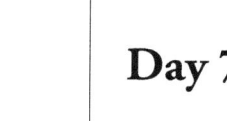

Day 7

Date: _____

- ○ Exodus 20:12
- ○ Exodus 21:17
- ○ Matthew 15:3-6
- ○ Isaiah 29:13-16
- ○ Malachi 1:6-14
- ○ Matthew 15:7-9
- ○ Proverbs 18:20-21
- ○ Proverbs 10:10-14
- ○ Matthew 15:10-11
- ○ Isaiah 5:24
- ○ Matthew 15:13
- ○ Deuteronomy 27:18
- ○ Isaiah 56:9-12
- ○ Matthew 15:14
- ○ Matthew 15:16-20
- ○ Matthew 15:24
- ○ Matthew 15:26
- ○ Matthew 15:28
- ○ Matthew 15:32
- ○ Matthew 15:34
- ○ Matthew 16:2-4
- ○ Matthew 16:6
- ○ Matthew 16:8-11
- ○ Matthew 16:13
- ○ Matthew 16:15
- ○ Matthew 16:17-19
- ○ Matthew 16:23
- ○ Matthew 16:24-28
- ○ Matthew 17:7
- ○ Matthew 17:9

To Whom is Jesus Speaking? _____

Where is He? _____

Time References? _____

Notes/Verses/Thoughts:
_____
_____
_____
_____
_____
_____
_____
_____
_____
_____
_____
_____
_____
_____
_____
_____
_____
_____
_____
_____
_____
_____
_____

(Continued)

- Matthew 17:11-12
- Deuteronomy 32:1-6
- Matthew 17:17
- Matthew 17:20-21
- Matthew 17:22-23
- Matthew 17:25
- Matthew 17:26
- Matthew 17:27
- Matthew 18:3-9
- Psalm 91:11-12
- Matthew 18:10-14

Notes/Verses/Thoughts:

Day 8

Date: _____

- Leviticus 19:17
- Matthew 18:15-20
- Matthew 18:23-35
- Malachi 2:10-16
- Matthew 19:4-6
- Matthew 19:8-9
- Matthew 19:11-12
- Matthew 19:14
- Matthew 19:17
- Leviticus 18:1-5
- Exodus 20:12-16
- Matthew 19:18-19
- Matthew 19:21
- Ezekiel 33:30-33
- Matthew 19:23-24
- Jeremiah 32:17
- Matthew 19:26
- Matthew 19:28-30
- Leviticus 19:13
- Matthew 20:1-16
- Matthew 20:18-19
- Matthew 20:21
- Matthew 20:22
- Psalm 116:12-19
- Matthew 20:23
- Matthew 20:25-28
- Isaiah 42:1-4
- Isaiah 44:22
- Matthew 20:32
- Matthew 21:2-3

To Whom is Jesus Speaking?
_____

Where is He?
_____

Time References?
_____

Notes/Verses/Thoughts:
_____
_____
_____
_____
_____
_____
_____
_____
_____
_____
_____
_____
_____
_____
_____
_____
_____
_____
_____
_____
_____
_____
_____

(Continued)

- Zechariah 9:9
- Matthew 21:13
- Jeremiah 7:1-29
- Matthew 21:16
- Psalm 8
- Matthew 21:19
- Matthew 21:21-22
- Matthew 21:24-25
- Matthew 21:27
- Matthew 21:28-31a
- Jeremiah 5:21-24
- Matthew 21:31b-32
- Isaiah 5:1-7
- Matthew 21:33-40
- Jeremiah 18:1-12
- Psalm 118:22-29
- Matthew 21:42-44

Notes/Verses/Thoughts:

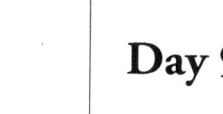

Day 9

Date: _____

- ○ Psalm 80
- ○ Matthew 22:2-3
- ○ Jeremiah 8:4-9
- ○ Matthew 22:4-11
- ○ Isaiah 61:10-11
- ○ Matthew 22:12-13
- ○ Isaiah 8:6-8
- ○ Zephaniah 1:7
- ○ Matthew 22:14
- ○ Matthew 22:18-21
- ○ Matthew 22:29-31
- ○ Exodus 3:6
- ○ Matthew 22:32
- ○ Joshua 22:5
- ○ Deutoronomy 4:29-31
- ○ Matthew 22:37-40
- ○ Matthew 22:42-43
- ○ Psalm 110
- ○ Matthew 22:44-45

To Whom is Jesus Speaking?
_____

Where is He?
_____

Time References?
_____

Notes/Verses/Thoughts:
_____
_____
_____
_____
_____
_____
_____
_____
_____
_____
_____
_____
_____
_____
_____
_____
_____
_____
_____
_____
_____
_____
_____
_____

The Messiah

Day 10

Date: _____

- ☐ Psalm 12
- ☐ Matthew 23:2-3
- ☐ Ezekiel 34:17-23
- ☐ Matthew 23:4-5
- ☐ Numbers 15:38-41
- ☐ Matthew 23:6
- ☐ Jeremiah 4:1-2
- ☐ Matthew 23:7-9
- ☐ Jeremiah 6:13-14
- ☐ Jeremiah 31:34
- ☐ Psalm 25:1-5
- ☐ Matthew 23:10
- ☐ 1 Samuel 2:1-9
- ☐ Proverb 3:35
- ☐ Matthew 23:11-12
- ☐ Malachi 2:1-9
- ☐ Matthew 23:13-14
- ☐ Isaiah 9:14-16
- ☐ Matthew 23:15
- ☐ Isaiah 10:1-2
- ☐ Exodus 29:37
- ☐ Matthew 23:16
- ☐ Psalm 11:1-5
- ☐ Matthew 23:17-22
- ☐ Proverbs 30:11-14
- ☐ Matthew 23:23-33
- ☐ Ezekiel 3:17-21
- ☐ Matthew 23:34
- ☐ Genesis 4:8
- ☐ 2 Chronicles 24:20-22

To Whom is Jesus Speaking?
_____

Where is He?
_____

Time References?
_____

Notes/Verses/Thoughts:
_____
_____
_____
_____
_____
_____
_____
_____
_____
_____
_____
_____
_____
_____
_____
_____
_____
_____
_____
_____
_____
_____

(Continued)

- Matthew 23:35-36
- Psalm 14
- Micah 2:6-13
- Matthew 23:37
- Zechariah 11:4-11
- Proverbs 11
- Matthew 23:38
- Zechariah 11:14-17
- Hosea 5:15
- Matthew 23:39
- Daniel 4:4-37
- Malachi 1:1-5
- Isaiah 6:11-13
- Matthew 24:2

Notes/Verses/Thoughts:

The Messiah

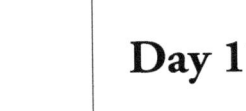

Day 11

Date: _____

- o   Matthew 24:4-21
- o   Joel 2:1-11
- o   Matthew 24:22-23
- o   Exodus 7:10-13
- o   Matthew 24:24-28
- o   Zephaniah 1:14-18
- o   Isaiah 29:5-8
- o   Matthew 24:29
- o   Zechariah 9:14-17
- o   Isaiah 27:12-13
- o   Matthew 24:30-37
- o   Genesis 7:6-24
- o   Matthew 24:38-51

To Whom is Jesus Speaking?
_____

Where is He?
_____

Time References?
_____

Notes/Verses/Thoughts:
_____
_____
_____
_____
_____
_____
_____
_____
_____
_____
_____
_____
_____
_____
_____
_____
_____
_____
_____
_____
_____
_____
_____
_____
_____
_____

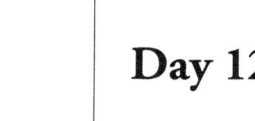

Day 12

Date: _____

- ○ Matthew 25:1-34
- ○ Isaiah 58:9b-14
- ○ Matthew 25:35-45
- ○ Proverb 14:31
- ○ Matthew 25:46
- ○ Matthew 26:2
- ○ Matthew 26:10-13
- ○ Matthew 26:18
- ○ Matthew 26:21
- ○ Matthew 26:23-24
- ○ Daniel 9:26
- ○ Matthew 26:25
- ○ Zechariah 11:12-13
- ○ Matthew 26:26
- ○ Exodus 24:1-12
- ○ Zechariah 9:11
- ○ Matthew 26:27-29
- ○ Zechariah 13:7
- ○ Matthew 26:31-32
- ○ Matthew 26:34
- ○ Matthew 26:36
- ○ Matthew 26:38-42
- ○ Matthew 26:45-46
- ○ Matthew 26:50
- ○ Matthew 26:52
- ○ 2 Kings 6:16-17
- ○ Matthew 26:53-54
- ○ Hosea 7:2-16
- ○ Matthew 26:55-56
- ○ Matthew 26:64
- ○ Matthew 26:75

To Whom is Jesus Speaking? _____

Where is He? _____

Time References? _____

Notes/Verses/Thoughts:
_____
_____
_____
_____
_____
_____
_____
_____
_____
_____
_____
_____
_____
_____
_____
_____
_____
_____
_____
_____
_____
_____

The Messiah

Day 13

Date: _____

- o Matthew 27:11
- o Matthew 27:46
- o Micah 7:8-10
    * unfortunate NIV translation. Should be: Though I bear the blame against him.
- o Matthew 28:9
- o Matthew 28:10
- o Isaiah 49:1-7
- o Daniel 7:13-14
- o Matthew 28:18-20
- o Daniel 6:26-27

To Whom is Jesus Speaking?
_____

Where is He?
_____

Time References?
_____

Notes/Verses/Thoughts:
_____
_____
_____
_____
_____
_____
_____
_____
_____
_____
_____
_____
_____
_____
_____
_____
_____
_____
_____
_____

Reflections

"A voice of one calling: 'In the desert prepare the way for the LORD; make straight in the wilderness a highway for our God, Every valley shall be raised up, every mountain and hill be made low; the rough ground shall become level, the rugged places a plain. And the glory of the LORD will be revealed, and all mankind together will see it. For the mouth of the LORD has spoken."

Isaiah 40:3-5 NIV

The Book of Mark

Day 14

Date: _____

- ○ Mark 1:15
- ○ Mark 1:17
- ○ Mark 1:25
- ○ Mark 1:38
- ○ Mark 1:41
- ○ Mark 1:44
- ○ Mark 2:5
- ○ Mark 2:8-11
- ○ Mark 2:14
- ○ Mark 2:17
- ○ Mark 2:19-22
- ○ Mark 2:24
- ○ Mark 2:25-26
- ○ Exodus 20:8-11
- ○ Exodus 23:12
- ○ Mark 2:27
- ○ Mark 3:3
- ○ Mark 3:4
- ○ Mark 3:5
- ○ Mark 3:23-29
- ○ Mark 3:33-35
- ○ Mark 4:3-9
- ○ Mark 4:11-12
- ○ Isaiah 6:9-10
- ○ Mark 4:13-20
- ○ Mark 4:21-25
- ○ Mark 4:26-29
- ○ Mark 4:30-32
- ○ Mark 4:35
- ○ Mark 4:39

To Whom is Jesus Speaking?
_____

Where is He?
_____

Time References?
_____

Notes/Verses/Thoughts:
_____
_____
_____
_____
_____
_____
_____
_____
_____
_____
_____
_____
_____
_____
_____
_____
_____
_____
_____
_____
_____
_____
_____
_____

(Continued)

- Mark 4:40
- Mark 5:8
- Mark 5:19
- Mark 5:30
- Mark 5:31
- Mark 5:34
- Mark 5:36
- Mark 5:39
- Mark 5:41
- Mark 6:4
- Mark 6:8-11
- Mark 6:31
- Mark 6:37
- Mark 6:38
- 2 Kings 4:42-44
- Mark 6:50
- Mark 7:6-13
- Proverbs 30:5-6
- Mark 7:14-23
- Mark 7:27
- Mark 7:29
- Mark 7:34

Notes/Verses/Thoughts:

Day 15

Date: _____

- ○ Mark 8:2-3
- ○ Mark 8:5
- ○ Mark 8:12
- ○ Mark 8:15
- ○ Mark 8:17-21
- ○ Mark 8:23
- ○ Mark 8:26
- ○ Mark 8:27
- ○ Mark 8:29
- ○ Mark 8:33-38
- ○ Mark 9:1
- ○ Mark 9:12-13
- ○ Mark 9:16
- ○ Mark 9:19
- ○ Mark 9:21
- ○ Mark 9:23
- ○ Mark 9:25
- ○ Mark 9:29
- ○ Mark 9:31
- ○ Mark 9:33
- ○ Mark 9:35
- ○ Mark 9:37
- ○ Mark 9:39-48
- ○ Isaiah 66:22-24
- ○ Mark 9:49-50
- ○ Leviticus 2:13
- ○ 2 Kings 2:19-22
- ○ Mark 10:3
- ○ Mark 10:5-9
- ○ Mark 10:11-12

To Whom is Jesus Speaking?
_____

Where is He?
_____

Time References?
_____

Notes/Verses/Thoughts:
_____
_____
_____
_____
_____
_____
_____
_____
_____
_____
_____
_____
_____
_____
_____
_____
_____
_____
_____
_____
_____
_____
_____
_____
_____

(Continued)

- Mark 10:14-15
- Mark 10:18-19
- Mark 10:21
- Psalm 52:7
- Mark 10:23
- Mark 10:24-25
- Mark 10:27
- Mark 10:29-31
- Mark 10:33-34
- Mark 10:36
- Mark 10:38
- Mark 10:39-40
- Mark 10:42-45
- Mark 10:49
- Mark 10:51-52
- Mark 11:2-3
- Mark 11:14
- Mark 11:17
- Isaiah 56:7
- Mark 11:22-26
- Mark 11:29-30
- Mark 11:33
- Mark 12:1-11
- Mark 12:15-17
- Mark 12:24-26
- Exodus 4:5
- Mark 12:27
- Mark 12:29-30
- Deuteronomy 6:4-9
- Mark 12:31
- Mark 12:34
- Mark 12:35-40
- Mark 12:43-44

Notes/Verses/Thoughts:

Day 16

Date: _____

- o Mark 13:2
- o Mark 13:5
- o Jeremiah 29:8-9
- o Deuteronomy 13:1-5
- o Mark 13:6-14
- o Daniel 9:26-27
- o Daniel 11:30-38
- o Daniel 12:11-12
- o Mark 13:15-19
- o Hosea 3:4-5
- o Joel 2:1-2
- o Daniel 12:1-4
- o Mark 13:20-25
- o Isaiah 13:9-13
- o Mark 13:26-27
- o Zechariah 2
- o Mark 13:28-37
- o Mark 14:6-9
- o Mark 14:13-15
- o Mark 14:18
- o Mark 14:20-21
- o Mark 14:22
- o Mark 14:24-25
- o Mark 14:27-28
- o Mark 14:30
- o Mark 14:32
- o Mark 14:34
- o Mark 14:36

To Whom is Jesus Speaking?
_____

Where is He?
_____

Time References?
_____

Notes/Verses/Thoughts:
_____
_____
_____
_____
_____
_____
_____
_____
_____
_____
_____
_____
_____
_____
_____
_____
_____
_____
_____
_____
_____
_____
_____
_____
_____
_____

(Continued)

The Suffering Servant

- Psalm 16
- Mark 14:37-38
- Isaiah 52:1-3
- Mark 14:41-42

Notes/Verses/Thoughts:

Day 17

Date: _____

- ○ Mark 14:48-49
- ○ Isaiah 53
- ○ Mark 14:62
- ○ Daniel 7:13-14
- ○ Mark 14:72
- ○ Mark 15:2
- ○ Mark 15:34
- ○ Psalm 22
- ○ Mark 16:15-18

To Whom is Jesus Speaking?
_____

Where is He?
_____

Time References?
_____

Notes/Verses/Thoughts:
_____
_____
_____
_____
_____
_____
_____
_____
_____
_____
_____
_____
_____
_____
_____
_____
_____
_____
_____
_____
_____
_____
_____

The Suffering Servant

Reflections

"When your words came, I ate them; they were my joy and
my heart's delight, for I bear your name,
O LORD God Almighty."

Jeremiah 15:16

The Book of Luke

Day 18

Date: _____

- o Luke 2:49
- o Luke 4:4
- o Deuteronomy 8:3
- o Luke 4:8
- o Luke 4:12
- o Luke 4:18-19
- o Isaiah 61:1-3
- o Isaiah 49:8-9
- o Luke 4:21
- o Luke 4:23-25
- o 1 Kings 17:1
- o 1 Kings 18:1
- o Luke 4:26
- o 1 Kings 17:8-16
- o Luke 4:27
- o 2 Kings 5:1-16
- o Luke 4:35
- o Luke 4:43
- o Luke 5:4
- o Luke 5:10
- o Luke 5:13-14
- o Luke 5:20
- o Luke 5:22-24
- o Luke 5:27
- o Luke 5:31-32
- o Luke 5:34-39
- o Luke 6:3-5
- o Luke 6:8-10
- o Luke 6:20-22
- o Isaiah 51:1-11

To Whom is Jesus Speaking?
_____

Where is He?
_____

Time References?
_____

Notes/Verses/Thoughts:
_____
_____
_____
_____
_____
_____
_____
_____
_____
_____
_____
_____
_____
_____
_____
_____
_____
_____
_____
_____
_____
_____
_____
_____

(Continued)

- Isaiah 30:7
- Luke 6:23-26
- Isaiah 65:8-16
- Luke 6:27-30
- Deuteronomy 15:7-8
- Proverb 21:26
- Luke 6:31-38
- Isaiah 65:6-7
- Luke 6:39-45
- Proverbs 4:20-27
- Luke 6:46-49

Notes/Verses/Thoughts:
_____
_____
_____
_____
_____
_____
_____
_____
_____
_____
_____
_____
_____
_____
_____
_____
_____
_____
_____
_____
_____
_____
_____
_____
_____
_____
_____
_____
_____

Day 19

Date: _____

- Luke 7:9
- Luke 7:13-14
- Luke 7:22
- Isaiah 29:9-12
- Isaiah 29:18-19
- Luke 7:23-28
- Luke 7:31-35
- Luke 7:40-44
- Genesis 18:1-5
- Genesis 43:24
- Judges 19:21
- Luke 7:45-46
- Psalm 23
- Luke 7:47-48
- Luke 7:50
- Luke 8:5-8
- Luke 8:10-15
- Luke 8:16-18
- Luke 8:21
- Luke 8:22
- Luke 8:25
- Luke 8:30
- Luke 8:39
- Luke 8:45-46
- Luke 8:48
- Luke 8:50
- Luke 8:52
- Luke 8:54
- Luke 9:3-5
- Luke 9:13-14

To Whom is Jesus Speaking? _____

Where is He? _____

Time References? _____

Notes/Verses/Thoughts:
_____
_____
_____
_____
_____
_____
_____
_____
_____
_____
_____
_____
_____
_____
_____
_____
_____
_____
_____
_____
_____
_____
_____

(Continued)

- Luke 9:18
- Luke 9:20
- Luke 9:22-27
- Luke 9:41
- Luke 9:44
- Luke 9:48
- Luke 9:50
- Luke 9:58-60
- Luke 9:62
- Luke 10:2-16
- Luke 10:18
- Isaiah 14:12-15
- Luke 10:19-24
- Luke 10:26
- Luke 10:28
- Luke 10:30-37
- Luke 10:41-42
- Psalm 27

Notes/Verses/Thoughts:

Day 20

Date: _____

- ☐ Luke 11:2-13
- ☐ Proverbs 8:1-11
- ☐ Luke 11:17-20
- ☐ Exodus 8:16-19
- ☐ Luke 11:21-26
- ☐ Luke 11:28
- ☐ Proverbs 8:31-36
- ☐ Luke 11:29-31
- ☐ 1 Kings 10:1-9
- ☐ Luke 11:32
- ☐ Luke 11:33-36
- ☐ Luke 11:39-42
- ☐ Micah 6:6-8
- ☐ Luke 11:43-44
- ☐ Numbers 19:16
- ☐ Luke 11:46-52
- ☐ Luke 12:1-7
- ☐ Psalm 84
- ☐ Luke 12:8-12
- ☐ Exodus 4:11-12
- ☐ Luke 12:14-15
- ☐ Psalm 62:9-10
- ☐ Luke 12:16-21
- ☐ Psalm 39:4-7
- ☐ Luke 12:22-31
- ☐ Psalm 147:1-14
- ☐ Luke 12:32-34
- ☐ Luke 12:35-48
- ☐ Luke 12:49-53
- ☐ Luke 12:54-59

To Whom is Jesus Speaking? _____

Where is He? _____

Time References? _____

Notes/Verses/Thoughts:
_____
_____
_____
_____
_____
_____
_____
_____
_____
_____
_____
_____
_____
_____
_____
_____
_____
_____
_____
_____

Day 21

Date: _____

- Luke 13:2-9
- Luke 13:12
- Luke 13:15-16
- Luke 13:18-21
- Luke 13:24
- Job 24:13
- Job 23:3-7
- Luke 13:25-27
- Psalm 9:7-10
- Luke 13:28-30
- Luke 13:32-35
- Luke 14:3
- Luke 14:5
- Luke 14:8-10
- Proverbs 29:23
- Isaiah 57:15
- Luke 14:11-14
- Proverb 22:9
- Luke 14:16-18
- Ecclesiastes 2:17-26
- Luke 14:19
- Ecclesiastes 2:4-11
- Luke 14:20
- Deuteronomy 4:16
- Luke 14:21-24
- Luke 14:26-34
- Numbers 18:19

To Whom is Jesus Speaking?
_____

Where is He?
_____

Time References?
_____

Notes/Verses/Thoughts:
_____
_____
_____
_____
_____
_____
_____
_____
_____
_____
_____
_____
_____
_____
_____
_____
_____
_____
_____
_____
_____
_____
_____
_____

(Continued)

- 2 Chronicles 13:5
- 1 Chronicles 17:4-14
- 2 Chronicles 7:11-22
- Luke 14:35

Notes/Verses/Thoughts:

Day 22

Date: _____

- ○ Luke 15:4
- ○ Psalm 119:169-176
- ○ Ezekiel 34:11-16
- ○ Luke 15:5-13
- ○ Hosea 2:5
- ○ Luke 15:14
- ○ Hosea 2:6
- ○ Luke 15:15-16
- ○ Hosea 2:7-10
- ○ Luke 15:17-19
- ○ Hosea 2:14
- ○ Luke 15:20-22
- ○ Hosea 2:15-23
- ○ Luke 15:23-24
- ○ Hosea 2:5-23
- ○ Luke 15:25-32
- ○ Malachi 3:6-18

To Whom is Jesus Speaking? _____

Where is He? _____

Time References? _____

Notes/Verses/Thoughts:
_____

The Son of Man

Day 23

Date: _____

- ○ Luke 16:1
- ○ Psalm 33:13-15
- ○ Luke 16:2-3
- ○ Proverbs 21:25-26
- ○ Ecclesiastes 4:4
- ○ Luke 16:4-5
- ○ Proverb 16:18
- ○ Ecclesiastes 7:7-8
- ○ Luke 16:6-7
- ○ Psalm 33:16-17
- ○ Ecclesiastes 3:9-12
- ○ Luke 16:8
- ○ Ecclesiastes 8:12-13
- ○ Psalm 17:1-6
- ○ Psalm 17:14
- ○ Proverbs 31:10-31
- ○ Luke 16:9
- ○ Job 14:11-17
- ○ Proverbs 15:3-9
- ○ Job 11:13-20
- ○ Job 16:19-22
- ○ Daniel 12:2-3
- ○ Psalm 17:15
- ○ Luke 16:10
- ○ Isaiah 33:6
- ○ Luke 16:11
- ○ Ecclesiastes 5:15-20
- ○ Luke 16:12

To Whom is Jesus Speaking?
_____

Where is He?
_____

Time References?
_____

Notes/Verses/Thoughts:
_____
_____
_____
_____
_____
_____
_____
_____
_____
_____
_____
_____
_____
_____
_____
_____
_____
_____
_____
_____
_____
_____
_____
_____

(Continued)

- Ecclesiastes 2:13-16
- Ecclesiastes 9:5-10
- Luke 16:13
- Psalm 86:11-13
- Luke 16:15
- Psalm 33:18-22
- Luke 16:16-31
- Psalm 37:35-40

Notes/Verses/Thoughts:

The Son of Man

Day 24

Date: _____

- ○ Luke 17:1-4
- ○ Luke 17:6-10
- ○ Luke 17:14
- ○ Luke 17:17-19
- ○ Luke 17:20-27
- ○ Genesis 6:1-8
- ○ Luke 17:28
- ○ Genesis 19:1-28
- ○ Luke 17:29-37
- ○ Luke 18:2-7
- ○ Exodus 22:22-23
- ○ Psalm 88:1-2
- ○ Luke 18:8
- ○ Malachi 2:17
- ○ Luke 18:10-12
- ○ Isaiah 65:1-5
- ○ Malachi 3:2-5
- ○ Luke 18:13-14
- ○ Psalm 19:12-14
- ○ Luke 18:16-17
- ○ Luke 18:19-20
- ○ Deuteronomy 5:16-20
- ○ Luke 18:22
- ○ Luke 18:24
- ○ Proverb 11:28
- ○ Luke 18:25
- ○ Luke 18:27
- ○ Luke 18:29-30
- ○ Deuteronomy 8:10-20
- ○ Luke 18:31-33
- ○ Luke 18:41-42

To Whom is Jesus Speaking?
_____

Where is He?
_____

Time References?
_____

Notes/Verses/Thoughts:
_____
_____
_____
_____
_____
_____
_____
_____
_____
_____
_____
_____
_____
_____
_____
_____
_____
_____
_____
_____
_____
_____

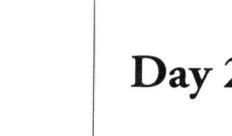

Day 25

Date: _____

- Luke 19:5
- Luke 19:9-10
- Luke 19:12-27
- Luke 19:30-31
- Luke 19:40
- Luke 19:42
- Isaiah 22:4
- Luke 19:43
- Ezekiel 3:27-4:3
- Luke 19:44
- Luke 19:46
- Deuteronomy 28:49-52
- Luke 20:3
- Luke 20:8
- Luke 20:9-18
- Isaiah 8:13-18
- Luke 20:24-25
- Luke 20:34-38
- Luke 20:41-43
- 1 Chronicles 22:5-13
- 1 Chronicles 28:2-13
- 1 Kings 5:3
- Luke 20:44
- Luke 20:46-47
- Luke 21:3-4
- Luke 21:8-10
- Isaiah 19:1-8

To Whom is Jesus Speaking? _____

Where is He? _____

Time References? _____

Notes/Verses/Thoughts:
_____
_____
_____
_____
_____
_____
_____
_____
_____
_____
_____
_____
_____
_____
_____
_____
_____
_____
_____
_____
_____
_____
_____
_____
_____

The Son of Man

Day 26

Date: _____

- ○ Luke 21:11-22
- ○ Hosea 9:7-12
- ○ Luke 21:23-24
- ○ Isaiah 63:18-19
- ○ Luke 21:25-36
- ○ Luke 22:8-12
- ○ Luke 22:15-20
- ○ Jeremiah 31:31-37
- ○ Luke 22:21-22
- ○ Luke 22:25-31
- ○ Job 1:6-12
- ○ Luke 22:32-38
- ○ Luke 22:40
- ○ Luke 22:42
- ○ Psalm 42
- ○ Luke 22:46
- ○ Luke 22:48
- ○ Luke 22:51
- ○ Luke 22:52-53
- ○ Isaiah 5:20-21
- ○ Luke 22:61
- ○ Micah 2:1
- ○ Luke 22:67-69
- ○ Isaiah 52:5-6
- ○ Luke 22:70

To Whom is Jesus Speaking?
_____

Where is He?
_____

Time References?
_____

Notes/Verses/Thoughts:
_____
_____
_____
_____
_____
_____
_____
_____
_____
_____
_____
_____
_____
_____
_____
_____
_____
_____
_____
_____
_____
_____
_____
_____

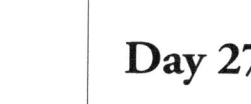

Day 27

Date: _____

- Luke 23:3
- Luke 23:28
- Micah 2:3-5
- Luke 23:29-30
- Hosea 10:8-10
- Luke 23:31
- Luke 23:34
- Luke 23:43
- Isaiah 50:4-11
- Luke 23:46
- Luke 24:7
- Luke 24:17
- Luke 24:19
- Luke 24:25-26
- Isaiah 52:7-15
- Luke 24:36-39
- Luke 24:41
- Luke 24:44
- Psalm 2
- Genesis 3:15
- Isaiah 7:13-14

To Whom is Jesus Speaking?
_____

Where is He?
_____

Time References?
_____

Notes/Verses/Thoughts:
_____
_____
_____
_____
_____
_____
_____
_____
_____
_____
_____
_____
_____
_____
_____
_____
_____
_____
_____
_____
_____
_____
_____
_____
_____
_____
_____

Reflections

"Your hands made me and formed me; give me understanding to learn your commands. May those who fear you rejoice when they see me, for I have put my hope in your word."

Psalm 119:73-74

The Book of John

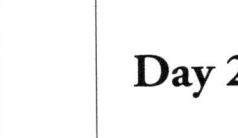

Day 28

Date: _____

- ○ John 1:37
- ○ John 1:39
- ○ John 1:42
- ○ John 1:43
- ○ John 1:47
- ○ Psalm 32
- ○ John 1:48
- ○ John 1:50-51
- ○ Genesis 28:10-13
- ○ John 2:4
- ○ John 2:7-8
- ○ John 2:16
- ○ Psalm 69:8-9
- ○ John 2:19
- ○ Jonah 1:17-2:10
- ○ John 3:3
- ○ Ezekiel 18:30-32
- ○ John 3:5-8
- ○ John 3:10-13
- ○ Proverbs 30:1-4
- ○ John 3:14-15
- ○ Numbers 21:8-9
- ○ John 3:16
- ○ Genesis 22:1-14
- ○ John 3:17-19
- ○ Genesis 1:1-4
- ○ John 3:20-21
- ○ Isaiah 9:1-7

To Whom is Jesus Speaking?
_____

Where is He?
_____

Time References?
_____

Notes/Verses/Thoughts:
_____
_____
_____
_____
_____
_____
_____
_____
_____
_____
_____
_____
_____
_____
_____
_____
_____
_____
_____
_____
_____
_____
_____

Day 29

Date: _____

- John 4:7
- John 4:10
- Jeremiah 2:13
- John 4:13-14
- Ezekiel 36:25-29
- Isaiah 12:2-6
- John 4:16-18
- John 4:21-24
- John 4:26
- John 4:32
- Job 23:12
- John 4:34-38
- Micah 6:15
- John 4:48
- Daniel 4:1-3
- John 4:50
- John 4:53
- John 5:6
- John 5:8
- John 5:11
- John 5:14
- John 5:17
- John 5:19-30
- John 5:31-38
- Isaiah 26:7-13
- John 5:39-40
- Numbers 14:11
- John 5:41-45
- Deuteronomy 30:11-20
- John 5:46-47

To Whom is Jesus Speaking?
_____

Where is He?
_____

Time References?
_____

Notes/Verses/Thoughts:
_____
_____
_____
_____
_____
_____
_____
_____
_____
_____
_____
_____
_____
_____
_____
_____
_____
_____
_____
_____
_____
_____

The Great I Am

Day 30

Date: _____

- ○ John 6:5
- ○ John 6:10
- ○ John 6:12
- ○ John 6:20
- ○ John 6:26-27
- ○ John 6:29
- ○ John 6:32-33
- ○ Numbers 11:7-9
- ○ Exodus 16:4
- ○ Nehemiah 9:13-21
- ○ John 6:35-39
- ○ Isaiah 27:2-3
- ○ John 6:40-45
- ○ Isaiah 54:13
- ○ John 6:46-51
- ○ John 6:53-58
- ○ John 6:61-64
- ○ John 6:65
- ○ John 6:67
- ○ John 6:70
- ○ John 7:6-8
- ○ John 7:16-17
- ○ Psalm 25:8-15
- ○ John 7:18-19
- ○ John 7:21-23
- ○ Genesis 17:9-14
- ○ John 7:24
- ○ 1 Samuel 16:1-12
- ○ Isaiah 11:1-5

To Whom is Jesus Speaking?
_____

Where is He?
_____

Time References?
_____

Notes/Verses/Thoughts:
_____
_____
_____
_____
_____
_____
_____
_____
_____
_____
_____
_____
_____
_____
_____
_____
_____
_____
_____
_____
_____
_____
_____
_____

(Continued)

- John 7:28-29
- John 7:33-34
- John 7:36-38
- Isaiah 58:11

Notes/Verses/Thoughts:

Day 31

Date: _____

- John 8:7
- Leviticus 20:10
- Deuteronomy 17:2-7
- John 8:10-11
- John 8:12
- Proverbs 4:1-19
- John 8:14-19
- John 8:21-26
- John 8:28-29
- John 8:31-32
- John 8:34-41
- Jeremiah 23:9-11
- John 8:42-44
- Genesis 3:1-5
- John 8:45-47
- John 8:49-51
- John 8:54-56
- John 8:58
- Exodus 3:11-15
- John 9:3-5
- John 9:7
- John 9:35
- John 9:37
- John 9:39
- John 9:41
- John 10:1-5
- John 10:7-8
- Jeremiah 23:1-5
- Ezekiel 34:1-10
- John 10:9

To Whom is Jesus Speaking? _____

Where is He? _____

Time References? _____

Notes/Verses/Thoughts:
_____
_____
_____
_____
_____
_____
_____
_____
_____
_____
_____
_____
_____
_____
_____
_____
_____
_____
_____
_____
_____
_____

(Continued)

- Numbers 27:15-21
- John 10:10-11
- Ezekiel 34:23-24
- Isaiah 40:11
- John 10:12-16
- Isaiah 56:3-8
- John 10:17-18
- John 10:25-30
- John 10:32
- John 10:34
- Psalm 82
- Genesis 1:26
- Genesis 3:22
- John 10:35-36
- 2 Samuel 7:11b-16
- Psalm 89:19-29
- John 10:37-38

Notes/Verses/Thoughts:

The Great I Am

Day 32

Date: _____

- ○ John 11:4
- ○ John 11:7
- ○ John 11:9-11
- ○ John 11:14-15
- ○ John 11:23
- ○ John 11:25-26
- ○ John 11:34
- ○ John 11:39
- ○ John 11:40-44
- ○ John 12:7-8
- ○ Deuteronomy 15:11
- ○ John 12:9
- ○ John 12:23-28
- ○ John 12:30-32
- ○ John 12:34-36
- ○ Psalm 119:105-112
- ○ John 12:44-46
- ○ Isaiah 60:1-5
- ○ John 12:47-50
- ○ John 13:7-8
- ○ John 13:10
- ○ John 13:12-14
- ○ Psalm 41:1-2
- ○ John 13:15-17
- ○ Psalm 41:3-4
- ○ John 13:18
- ○ Psalm 41:5-13
- ○ Genesis 3:15
- ○ John 13:19-21

To Whom is Jesus Speaking? _____

Where is He? _____

Time References? _____

Notes/Verses/Thoughts:
_____
_____
_____
_____
_____
_____
_____
_____
_____
_____
_____
_____
_____
_____
_____
_____
_____
_____
_____
_____
_____
_____

(Continued)

- John 13:26-27
- John 13:31-35
- John 13:36
- John 13:38

Notes/Verses/Thoughts:

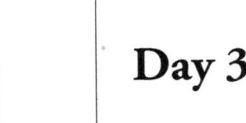

Day 33

Date: _____

- John 14:1-4
- Isaiah 26:19-20
- Psalm 27:5
- John 14:6
- Psalm 119:33-64
- John 14:7
- John 14:9-14
- Psalm 103
- John 14:15-21
- Deuteronomy 7:9-12
- Jeremiah 29:11-14
- John 14:23-27
- Numbers 6:24-26
- Psalm 85
- John 14:28-31
- John 15:1-21
- Isaiah 66:5
- Amos 5:10
- John 15:22-27

To Whom is Jesus Speaking?
_____

Where is He?
_____

Time References?
_____

Notes/Verses/Thoughts:
_____
_____
_____
_____
_____
_____
_____
_____
_____
_____
_____
_____
_____
_____
_____
_____
_____
_____
_____
_____
_____
_____
_____

Day 34

Date: _____

- ○ John 16:1-13
- ○ Psalm 25:4-5
- ○ John 16:14-20
- ○ Micah 4:6-9
- ○ John 16:21
- ○ Micah 4:10
- ○ John 16:22
- ○ Micah 4:11-14
- ○ Jeremiah 31:10-20
- ○ John 16:23-28
- ○ John 16:31-33
- ○ John 17:1-11
- ○ Psalm 133
- ○ John 17:12-13
- ○ Nehemiah 6:15
- ○ Nehemiah 7:1-3
- ○ Nehemiah 7:73
- ○ Nehemiah 8:1-2
- ○ Nehemiah 8:9-12
- ○ John 17:14-17
- ○ Psalm 19:7-11
- ○ Psalm 119:1-18
- ○ John 17:18-19
- ○ John 17:20-21
- ○ Jeremiah 32:38-39
- ○ John 17:22-26
- ○ John 18:4
- ○ John 18:5
- ○ John 18:6
- ○ John 18:7

To Whom is Jesus Speaking? _____

Where is He? _____

Time References? _____

Notes/Verses/Thoughts:
_____
_____
_____
_____
_____
_____
_____
_____
_____
_____
_____
_____
_____
_____
_____
_____
_____
_____
_____
_____
_____
_____
_____
_____

(Continued)

- John 18:8
- John 18:9
- John 18:11
- John 18:20-21
- John 18:23
- John 18:34
- John 18:36-37
- John 19:11
- John 19:26-27
- John 19:28
- John 19:30
- Daniel 9:24-26a
- John 20:15
- John 20:16
- John 20:17
- John 20:19
- John 20:21
- John 20:22-23
- John 20:26-27
- John 20:29
- John 21:5-6
- John 21:10
- John 21:12
- John 21:15-19
- John 21:22
- John 21:23

Notes/Verses/Thoughts:

Reflections

"We wait in hope for the LORD; he is our help and our shield. In him our hearts rejoice, for we trust in his holy name. May your unfailing love rest upon us, O LORD, even as we put our hope in you."

Psalm 33:20-22

ns,
Revelation
Acts, 1 Corinthians, 2 Corinthians, Revelation

Day 35

Date: _____

- ○ Acts 1:4-5
- ○ Acts 1:7
- ○ Deuteronomy 29:29
- ○ Acts 1:8
- ○ Acts 9:4-6
- ○ Acts 9:10-12
- ○ Acts 9:15-16
- ○ Acts 10:13
- ○ Acts 10:15
- ○ Genesis 9:3
- ○ Acts 11:7
- ○ Acts 11:9
- ○ Acts 11:16
- ○ Acts 18:9-10
- ○ Acts 20:35
- ○ Acts 22:7-8
- ○ Acts 22:10
- ○ Acts 22:18
- ○ Acts 22:21
- ○ Acts 23:11
- ○ Acts 26:14-17
- ○ Jeremiah 1:4-12
- ○ Acts 26:18
- ○ Isaiah 35:1-6
- ○ Psalm 18:28-50
- ○ Isaiah 42:6-7
- ○ Isaiah 42:16
- ○ Ezekiel 3:17-19
- ○ 1 Corinthians 11:24-25
- ○ 2 Corinthians 12:9

To Whom is Jesus Speaking?
_____

Where is He?
_____

Time References?
_____

Notes/Verses/Thoughts:
_____
_____
_____
_____
_____
_____
_____
_____
_____
_____
_____
_____
_____
_____
_____
_____
_____
_____
_____
_____
_____
_____

Day 36

Date: _____

- ○ Revelation 1:8
- ○ Isaiah 44:6-8
- ○ Revelation 1:11
- ○ Revelation 1:17
- ○ Ezekiel 1:25-28
- ○ Revelation 1:18
- ○ Job 19:23-27
- ○ Revelation 1:19-20

To Whom is Jesus Speaking?
_____

Where is He?
_____

Time References?
_____

Notes/Verses/Thoughts:
_____
_____
_____
_____
_____
_____
_____
_____
_____
_____
_____
_____
_____
_____
_____
_____
_____
_____
_____
_____
_____
_____
_____
_____
_____

The Great I Am

Day 37

Date: _____

- o Revelation 2:1-17
- o Isaiah 62:2-4
- o Revelation 2:18-20
- o 1 Kings 16:31
- o 1 Kings 21:23-29
- o 2 Kings 9:7-10
- o 2 Kings 9:30-37
- o Revelation 2:21-23
- o 1 Kings 8:38-40
- o Jeremiah 17:10
- o Psalm 139:1-19
- o Revelation 2:24-27
- o Psalm 2
- o Psalm 45:1-8
- o Isaiah 30:12-14
- o Ezekiel 21:25-32
- o Revelation 2:28-29

To Whom is Jesus Speaking?
_____

Where is He?
_____

Time References?
_____

Notes/Verses/Thoughts:
_____

Day 38

Date: _____

- Revelation 3:1-7
- Isaiah 22:20-25
- Revelation 3:8-9
- Isaiah 49:23
- Revelation 3:10-13
- Isaiah 65:17-25
- Revelation 3:14-17
- Hosea 12:1-8
- Revelation 3:18-19
- Deuteronomy 8:5
- Proverbs 3:11-12
- Revelation 3:20-22
- Job 42:1-6
- Psalm 72

To Whom is Jesus Speaking?
_____
Where is He?
_____
Time References?
_____
Notes/Verses/Thoughts:
_____

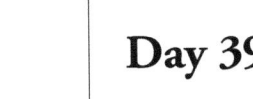

Day 39

Date: _____

- o Revelation 4:1
- o Joel 2:1-27
- o Revelation 16:15
- o Zechariah 12:10-14
- o Revelation 22:7
- o Joel 2:28-32
- o Revelation 22:12-14
- o Isaiah 62:5-12
- o Revelation 22:15
- o Isaiah 44:9-20
- o Isaiah 40:10-31
- o Revelation 22:16
- o Isaiah 44:21-28
- o Revelation 22:20

To Whom is Jesus Speaking?
_____

Where is He?
_____

Time References?
_____

Notes/Verses/Thoughts:
_____
_____
_____
_____
_____
_____
_____
_____
_____
_____
_____
_____
_____
_____
_____
_____
_____
_____
_____
_____
_____
_____

Day 40

Has your view of Jesus changed? Do you have a greater appreciation of His power? His love? His sacrifice?

OT References

Genesis
- 1:1-4.....Day 28
- 1:26.....Day 31
- 3:1-5.....Day 31
- 3:15.....Day 27, 32
- 3:22.....Day 31
- 4:8.....Day 10
- 6:1-8.....Day 24
- 7:6-24.....Day 11
- 9:3.....Day 35
- 17:9-14.....Day 30
- 18:1-5.....Day 19
- 19:1-28.....Day 24
- 22:1-14.....Day 28
- 28:10-13.....Day 28
- 43:24.....Day 19

Exodus
- 3:6.....Day 9
- 3:11-15.....Day 31
- 4:5.....Day 15
- 4:11-12.....Day 20
- 7:10-13.....Day 11
- 8:16-19.....Day 20
- 12:6-8.....Day 6
- 16:4.....Day 30
- 17:1-7.....Day 1
- 20:8-11.....Day 14
- 20:12.....Day 7
- 20:12-16.....Day 8
- 21:17.....Day 7
- 22:22-23.....Day 24
- 23:12.....Day 14
- 24:1-14.....Day 12
- 29:37.....Day 10
- 33:13-14.....Day 4

Leviticus
- 2:13.....Day 15
- 14:1-7.....Day 3
- 18:1-5.....Day 8
- 19:13.....Day 8
- 19:17.....Day 8
- 19:18.....Day 2
- 20:10.....Day 31
- 24:5-9.....Day 5
- 24:17-22.....Day 2

Numbers
- 6:24-26.....Day 33
- 11:7-9.....Day 30
- 14:11.....Day 29
- 15:38-41.....Day 10
- 18:19.....Day 21
- 19:16.....Day 20
- 21:8-9.....Day 28
- 27:15-21.....Day 31

Deuteronomy
- 4:16.....Day 21
- 4:29-31.....Day 9
- 5:16-20.....Day 24
- 6:4-9.....Day 15
- 6:13-16.....Day 1
- 7:9-12.....Day 33
- 8:3.....Day 18
- 8:5.....Day 38
- 8:10-20.....Day 24
- 13:1-5.....Day 16
- 15:7-8.....Day 18
- 15:11.....Day 32
- 17:2-7.....Day 31
- 19:15-21.....Day 2
- 23:21-23.....Day 1
- 24:1.....Day 1
- 27:18.....Day 7
- 28:49-52.....Day 25
- 29:2-15.....Day 6
- 29:29.....Day 35
- 30:11-20.....Day 29
- 32:1-6.....Day 7

Joshua
- 22:5.....Day 9

Judges
- 19:21.....Day 19

Samuels
- 1 Samuel 2:1-9.....Day 10
- 1 Samuel 16:1-12.....Day 30
- 1 Samuel 21:1-6.....Day 5
- 1 Samuel 25:5-6.....Day 4
- 2 Samuel 7:11b-16.....Day 31

Kings
- 1 Kings 5:3.....Day 25
- 1 Kings 8:38-40.....Day 37
- 1 Kings 10:1-9.....Day 20
- 1 Kings 16:31.....Day 37
- 1 Kings 17:1.....Day 18
- 1 Kings 17:8-16.....Day 18
- 1 Kings 18:1.....Day 18
- 1 Kings 21:23-29.....Day 37
- 2 Kings 2:19-22.....Day 15
- 2 Kings 4:1-7.....Day 6
- 2 Kings 4:42-44.....Day 14
- 2 Kings 5:1-16.....Day 18
- 2 Kings 6:16-17.....Day 12
- 2 Kings 9:7-10, 30-37.....Day 37

Chronicles
- 1 Ch. 16:8-36.....Day 5
- 1 Ch. 17:4-14 2.....Day 21
- 1 Ch. 22:5-13.....Day 25
- 1 Ch. 28:2-13.....Day 25
- 2 Ch. 7:11-22.....Day 21
- 2 Ch. 9:1-8.....Day 5
- 2 Ch. 13:5.....Day 21
- 2 Ch. 24:20-22.....Day 10

Nehemiah
- 6:15.....Day 34
- 7:1-3, 73.....Day 34
- 8:1-2, 9-12.....Day 34
- 9:13-21.....Day 30

Job
- 1:6-12.....Day 26
- 11:13-20.....Day 23
- 14:11-17.....Day 23
- 16:19-22.....Day 23
- 19:23-27.....Day 36
- 23:3-7.....Day 21
- 23:12.....Day 29
- 24:13.....Day 21
- 42:1-6.....Day 38

Psalms
- 2.....Day 27, 37
- 8.....Day 8
- 9:7-10.....Day 21
- 10:1-4.....Day 3
- 11:1-5.....Day 10
- 12.....Day 10
- 14.....Day 10
- 16.....Day 16
- 17:1-6, 14.....Day 23
- 17:15.....Day 23
- 18:28-50.....Day 35
- 19:7-11.....Day 34
- 19:12-14.....Day 24
- 22.....Day 17
- 23.....Day 19
- 24:1-6.....Day 1
- 25:1-5.....Day 10
- 25:4-5.....Day 34
- 25:8-15.....Day 30
- 27.....Day 19
- 27:5.....Day 33
- 32.....Day 28
- 33:13-15.....Day 23
- 33:16-17.....Day 23
- 33:18-22.....Day 23
- 37:1-34.....Day 1
- 37:35-40.....Day 23
- 39:4-7.....Day 20
- 41:1-2.....Day 1, 32
- 41:3-4.....Day 32
- 41:5-13.....Day 32
- 42.....Day 26
- 45:1-8.....Day 37
- 52:7.....Day 15
- 62:9-10.....Day 20
- 69:8-9.....Day 28
- 72.....Day 38
- 78:1-8.....Day 5
- 80.....Day 9
- 82.....Day 31
- 84.....Day 20
- 85.....Day 33
- 86:11-13.....Day 23
- 88:1-2.....Day 24
- 89:9.....Day 3
- 89:19-29.....Day 31
- 91:11-12.....Day 7
- 91:14-16.....Day 3
- 103.....Day 33
- 107:19-22.....Day 3
- 110.....Day 9
- 116:12-19.....Day 8
- 118:22-29.....Day 8
- 119:1-18.....Day 34
- 119:33-64.....Day 33
- 119:105-112.....Day 32
- 119:169-176.....Day 22
- 133.....Day 34
- 139:1-19.....Day 37
- 139:19-24.....Day 2
- 145:8-21.....Day 2
- 147:1-14.....Day 20

Proverbs
- 1:1-7.....Day 3
- 3:11-12.....Day 38
- 3:35.....Day 10
- 4:1-19.....Day 31
- 4:20-27.....Day 18
- 6:20-33.....Day 1
- 8:1-11.....Day 20
- 8:12-31.....Day 3
- 8:32-36.....Day 20
- 10:10-14.....Day 7
- 11.....Day 10
- 11:28.....Day 24
- 12:13-23.....Day 5
- 14:31.....Day 11
- 15:3-9.....Day 23
- 16:18.....Day 23
- 18:20-21.....Day 7
- 19:17.....Day 4
- 21:25-26.....Day 18, 23
- 22:9.....Day 21
- 23:4-5.....Day 2
- 29:23.....Day 21
- 30:1-4.....Day 28
- 30:5-6.....Day 14
- 30:7-9.....Day 2
- 30:11-14.....Day 10
- 31:10-31.....Day 23

Ecclesiastes
   2:4-11
   2:17-26
   2:13-16.....Day 23
   3:9-12.....Day 23
   4:4.....Day 23
   5:2-3, 7.....Day 1
   5:4-6.....Day 1
   5:15-20.....Day 23
   7:7-8.....Day 23
   8:12-13.....Day 23
   9:5-10.....Day 23

Isaiah
   2:2-6.....Day 29
   5:1-7.....Day 8
   5:20-21.....Day 26
   5:24.....Day 7
   6:8-10.....Day 1
   6:9-10.....Day 14
   6:11-13.....Day 10
   7:13-14.....Day 27
   8:6-8.....Day 9
   8:11-13.....Day 4
   8:13-18.....Day 25
   9:1-7.....Day 28
   9:14-16.....Day 10
   10:1-2.....Day 10
   11:1-5.....Day 30
   13:9-13.....Day 16
   14:12-15.....Day 19
   19:1-8.....Day 25
   22:4.....Day 25
   22:20-25.....Day 38
   26:7-13.....Day 29
   26:19-20.....Day 33
   27:2-3.....Day 30
   27:12-13.....Day 11

29:5-8.....Day 11
29:9-12, 18-19.....Day 19
29:13-16.....Day 7
30:7.....Day 18
30:12-14.....Day 37
32:17.....Day 1
33:6.....Day 23
35:1-6.....Day 35
40:6-9.....Day 1
40:10-31.....Day 39
40:11.....Day 31
42:1-4.....Day 8
42:6-7, 16.....Day 35
44:6-8.....Day 36
44:9-20.....Day 39
44:21-28.....Day 39
44:22.....Day 8
49:1-7.....Day 13
49:8-9.....Day 18
49:23.....Day 38
50:4-11.....Day 27
51:1-11.....Day 18
51:11-16.....Day 1
52:1-3.....Day 16
52:5-6.....Day 26
52:7-15.....Day 27
53.....Day 17
54:13.....Day 30
55.....Day 1
56:1-2.....Day 1
56:3-8.....Day 31
56:7.....Day 15
56:9-12.....Day 7
57:15.....Day 21
58:1-9a.....Day 2
58:9b-14.....Day 12
58:11.....Day 30
59:19-21.....Day 3

60:1-5.....Day 32
61:1-3.....Day 18
61:10-11.....Day 9
62:2-4.....Day 37
62:5-12.....Day 39
63:18-19.....Day 26
65:1-5.....Day 24
65:6-7.....Day 18
65:8-16.....Day 18
65:17-25.....Day 38
66:5.....Day 33
66:22-24.....Day 15

Jeremiah
   1:4-12.....Day 35
   2:13.....Day 29
   3:12-19.....Day 2
   4:1-2.....Day 10
   5:21-24.....Day 8
   5:26-28.....Day 6
   6:10.....Day 6
   6:13-14.....Day 10
   7:1-29.....Day 8
   8:4-9.....Day 9
   15:19.....Day 2
   17:10.....Day 37
   18:1-12.....Day 8
   23:1-5.....Day 31
   23:9-11.....Day 31
   23:16-29.....Day 3
   29:8-9.....Day 16
   29:11-14.....Day 3, 33
   31:10-20.....Day 34
   31:31-37.....Day 26
   31:34.....Day 10
   32:17.....Day 8
   32:38-39.....Day 34
   50:6.....Day 4

Ezekiel
- 1:25-28.....Day 36
- 3:17-19.....Day 35
- 3:17-21.....Day 10
- 3:27- 4:3.....Day 25
- 12:1-2.....Day 6
- 17:22-24.....Day 6
- 18:30-32.....Day 25
- 21:25-32.....Day 37
- 31:1-14.....Day 6
- 33:30-33.....Day 8
- 34:1-10.....Day 31
- 34:11-16.....Day 22
- 34:17-23.....Day 10
- 34:23-24.....Day 31
- 35:11.....Day 2
- 36:25-29.....Day 29

Daniel
- 4:1-3.....Day 29
- 4:4-37.....Day 10
- 6:26-27.....Day 13
- 7:13-14.....Day 13, 17
- 9:24-26a.....Day 34
- 9:26.....Day 12
- 9:26-27.....Day 16
- 11:30-38.....Day 16
- 12:1-4.....Day 16
- 12:2-3.....Day 23
- 12:11-12.....Day 16

Hosea
- 2:5-10, 14-23.....Day 22
- 3:4-5.....Day 16
- 5:15.....Day 10
- 6:1-6.....Day 4
- 7:2-16.....Day 12
- 8:1-5.....Day 3
- 9:7-12.....Day 26
- 10:3-10.....Day 27
- 12:1-8.....Day 38

Joel
- 2:1-2.....Day 16
- 2:1-11.....Day 11
- 2:1-27.....Day 39
- 2:28-32.....Day 39
- 3:13.....Day 6

Amos
- 1:9-10.....Day 4
- 5:10.....Day 33

Jonah
- 1:2.....Day 5
- 1:17.....Day 5
- 1:17-2:10.....Day 28
- 3:5.....Day 5

Micah
- 2:1.....Day 26
- 2:3-5.....Day 27
- 2:6-13.....Day 10
- 4:6-9.....Day 34
- 4:10.....Day 34
- 4:11-14.....Day 34
- 6:6-8.....Day 20
- 6:15.....Day 29
- 7:4-7.....Day 4
- 7:8-10.....Day 13

Zephaniah
- 1:7.....Day 9
- 1:14-18.....Day 11

Zechariah
- 2.....Day 16
- 7:5.....Day 2
- 8:19.....Day 2
- 9:9.....Day 8
- 9:11.....Day 12
- 9:14-17.....Day 11
- 11:4-11.....Day 10
- 11:12-13.....Day 12
- 11:14-17.....Day 10
- 12:10-14.....Day 39
- 13:7.....Day 12

Malachi
- 1:1-5.....Day 10
- 1:6-14.....Day 7
- 2:1-9.....Day 10
- 2:10-16.....Day 8
- 2:17.....Day 24
- 3:1.....Day 4
- 3:2-5.....Day 24
- 3:6-18.....Day 22
- 4:5-6.....Day 4

"Not only was the Teacher wise, be he also imparted knowledge to the people. He pondered and searched out and set in order many proverbs. The Teacher searched to find just the right words, and what he wrote was upright and true. The words of the wise are like goads, their collected saying like firmly embedded nails—given by one shepherd. Be warned, my son, of anything in addition to them. Of making many books there is no end, and much study wearies the body. Now all has been heard; here is the conclusion of the matter: Fear God and keep his commandments, for this is the duty of all mankind. For God will bring every deed into judgment, including every hidden thing, whether it is good or evil."

Ecclesiastes 12:9-14

www.ingramcontent.com/pod-product-compliance
Lightning Source LLC
Chambersburg PA
CBHW081253040426
42453CB00014B/2393